Table of Contents

I.	Key Observations of Terrorism Incidents Worldwide	2
II.	Foreword	5
III.	Interpreting the Data	6
IV.	Methodology for Determining Terrorist Incidents	7
	What is a "noncombatant"?	8
	What is "politically motivated violence"?	9
V.	General Observations of Worldwide Incidents of Terror	12
VI.	Charts Comparing 2005 and 2006	17-37
	Lethality – Fatalities and Incidents By Region	
	Attacks and Victims by Region	
	Methods Used in Fatality Incidents	
	Fatalities by Perpetrator	
	Fatalities by Victim Category	
	Top 15 Countries by Fatalities	
	Top 15 Countries by Hostages	
	Primary Methods Used in Attacks	
	Injuries By Weapon	
	All Attacks Involving Facilities or Vehicles	
	Iraq and non-Iraq Incidents	
VII.	Africa	38
VIII.	East Asia-Pacific	43
IX.	Europe-Eurasia	44
X.	Near East	45
XI.	South Asia	79
XII.	Western Hemisphere	91
	Appendix	
	Letter – Perspective Regarding Statistical Data	92

Foreword

Consistent with its statutory mission to serve as the US Government's knowledge bank on international terrorism, the National Counterterrorism Center (NCTC) is providing this report on incidents of terrorism to assist policymakers and the public, including terrorism experts and observers, in understanding the magnitude of the worldwide threat posed by terrorism. NCTC analyzes incidents of terror in direct support of the Department of State to assist it in satisfying annual reporting requirements under Section 2656f of title 22 of the US Code. The NCTC incident analysis, including individual incident records and statistical information, is available on the *www.nctc.gov* Web site.

Section 2656f(b) of Title 22 of the U.S. Code requires the State Department to include in its annual report on terrorism "to the extent practicable, complete statistical information on the number of individuals, including US citizens and dual nationals, killed, injured, or kidnapped by each terrorist group during the preceding calendar year." While NCTC records and keeps statistics on the annual number of incidents of "terrorism," its ability to track the specific groups responsible for each incident involving killings, kidnappings, and injuries is significantly limited by the availability of reliable open source information, particularly for events involving small numbers of casualties. Moreover, specific details about victims, damage, perpetrators, and other incident elements are frequently not fully reported in open source information.

- The statistical material in this report, therefore, is based upon the incidents of "terrorism" that occurred in 2006 as reported in open-source information, which is the most comprehensive body of information available to NCTC to meet the above-referenced statistical requirements.

In deriving its figures for incidents of terrorism, NCTC in 2005 and 2006 adopted the definition of "terrorism" that appears in 22 USC. § 2656f(d)(2) which defines terrorism as "premeditated, politically motivated violence perpetrated against noncombatant targets by subnational groups or clandestine agents."

- Through 2004 NCTC compiled statistical data on the basis of a more limited methodology tied to the definition of "international terrorism," which is also contained in 22 U.S.C. § 2656f.
- Because of the change in methodology, 2006 data are only comparable to the incident data compiled by NCTC for 2005.
- Subject to changes in reporting statutes, NCTC anticipates that future compilations will use the broader definition of "terrorism."

To record and update incident records, NCTC posts information in the repository for the U.S. Government's database on terrorist incidents, the Worldwide Incidents Tracking System (WITS), which was unveiled in 2005. A data management system with a more comprehensive dataset than those used in previous years, WITS is accessible on the NCTC Web site at *www.nctc.gov* for the public to have an open and transparent view of the NCTC data. NCTC will ensure that the data posted to the Web site are updated as often as practicable by regularly posting information about new or prior incidents.

Interpreting the Data

NCTC cautions against placing too much emphasis on any single set of incident data to gauge success or failure against the forces of terrorism. Further, NCTC does not believe that a simple comparison of the total number of incidents from year to year provides a meaningful measure.

- Tallying incident data necessarily involves relying exclusively on frequently incomplete and ambiguous information that is not derived from federal government collection programs created or operated specifically to obtain the data. The quality, accuracy, and volume of incident open source reporting can vary greatly from country to country. As a result, determining whether an incident meets the NCTC criteria for a terrorist incident is often difficult and highly subjective. This is particularly true if the incident does not involve mass casualties because little information is typically available on these incidents, which usually are not subject to heavy media coverage. Further, in the parts of the world where there is little press coverage and little nongovernmental organization presence, terrorist incidents go unreported.

- Incident tallies do not, by themselves, provide a complete picture of the magnitude or seriousness of the terrorism challenge confronting a country or region. For example, although 50 percent of the incidents in the NCTC database involve no loss of life, this data point would be only one factor in assessing the danger of terrorism globally. Moreover, different factors weigh more heavily than others in assessing the dangers posed by terrorism. For example, an attack that kills 100 civilians is likely to be considered more alarming than an attack that damages a pipeline but harms no one; however, each attack is simply tallied as one incident.

- Counting protocols matter and inevitably lead to judgment calls designating an event an act of terrorism. For example, NCTC protocols dictate that events identified as simultaneous and coordinated would be recorded as one incident, as would be attacks that subsequently targeted first-responders. For instance, on the morning of 17 August 2005, there were approximately 450 small bomb attacks in Bangladesh, and because they were coordinated according to a central plan, NCTC counted them as a single incident. Other valid counting protocols would register these attacks as 450 separate incidents.

- Analyzing incident data from year to year to identify trends and notable deviations in the data is problematic, and not meaningful in most cases. The availability, quality, and depth of open-source reporting vary, making it hard to isolate whether a rise or fall of a particular data element from one year to the next is due to an increase or decrease of this open source reporting or whether actual events are behind the change in the data.

Despite these limitations, tracking and analyzing incidents can help us understand some important characteristics about terrorism, including the geographic distribution of incidents and information about the perpetrators, their victims, and other details about an attack. Year-to-year changes in the gross number of incidents across the globe, however, may tell us little about the international community's effectiveness either for preventing these incidents, or for reducing the capacity of terrorists to advance their agenda through violence against the innocent.

Method for Determining Terrorist Incidents

After consulting with a panel of terrorism experts, NCTC in 2005 revised its methodology for determining terrorist incidents, basing it on the broader statutory definition of "*terrorism*" rather than that of "*international terrorism*,"[1] on which the NCTC based its incident counting in previous years. This broader definition, along with improvements in cataloging, has resulted in a larger and more comprehensive set of incident data.

The essential element of the statutory definition, found in 22 U.S.C. 2656f(d)(2), is that an incident must represent "premeditated, *politically motivated violence* perpetrated against *noncombatant targets* by subnational groups or clandestine agents." Determination of what constitutes an incident of terrorism is often subjective, however, because it is frequently based on incomplete information about an incident, including the perpetrator's specific motivation or identity.

NCTC strives to limit the degree of subjectivity for determining an incident and has developed specific criteria, which are continuously reviewed, to classify an attack as terrorism related. Organizations and experts, applying different criteria and perspectives, may differ on whether a particular incident constitutes terrorism or some

---

[1] Users who wish to determine the number of incidents of "international terrorism" (i.e., incidents that involve the territory or citizens of two or more countries) will find these incidents included in the WITS database.

other form of political violence. Moreover, organizations using both classified and unclassified information will almost certainly compile different tallies as well. Because there is such a diversity of methods and sources being used by organizations to compile incidents by country, group, or other categories, tallies of attacks for such places as Iraq and Afghanistan can, and often do, vary substantially.

Examples of Multiple Events Designated as One Incident of Terror

- In Chad during the 4-13 November 2006 time frame, assailants attacked 60 villages, killing over 400 people. Because the attacks were perpetrated by the same group at the same time as a campaign against the victims, the attacks were recorded as one incident.
- In Sudan on 29-30 October 2006, the Janjaweed Militia attacked nine communities, killing 63 people. Because the attacks were perpetrated by the same group at the same time as part of a campaign against the victims, the attacks were recorded as one incident.
- In Iraq on 3-4 October 2006, assailants set fire to 22 houses in the same general location. Because the attacks appeared to be coordinated to occur on the same days, in the same location as a campaign to target a specific community, the attacks were recorded as one incident.
- On 22 February In Samarra', Salah ad Din governorate, four assailants detonated two improvised explosive devices (IEDs) inside the Shiite Askariya (Golden Dome) Mosque, collapsing the dome and damaging the mosque's north wall. Reacting to this attack, on 22 and 23 February 2006, throughout Iraq, assailants attacked at least 184 Sunni mosques with grenades, small arms, mortars, and rocket-propelled grenades (RPGs), killing 12 Sunni imams and seven Sunni civilian worshippers, kidnapping 14 Sunni imams, and causing substantial damage to many of the mosques.

What Is a "Noncombatant"?

Under the statutory definition of *terrorism* that NCTC uses to compile its database, the victim must be a "noncombatant." However, that term is left open to interpretation by the statute. For the purposes of determining a terrorism incident and posting it to the WITS database, the term "combatant" is interpreted to mean personnel in the military, paramilitary, militia, and police under military command and control, who are in specific areas or regions where war zones or war-like settings exist.

- The fighting in 2006 between Hizballah—a US-designated foreign terrorist organization (FTO)—and Israeli forces in southern Lebanon during the summer of 2006 is considered by NCTC to have been between opposing combatant forces.

However, these entities are often not in combatant status; further distinctions are drawn depending on the particular country involved and the circumstances associated with these entities.

- Civilian police and military personnel that are victims of terrorism outside of war zones and war-like settings are considered noncombatants. These personnel are also considered noncombatant if they are victims of terrorism while they are off duty or conducting themselves as civilians in nongovernment settings. For example, personnel harmed during the Hizballah missile attacks on Israeli cities in 2006 fall into this category.

Government targets that are not exclusively military or security related, such as diplomatic personnel, embassies, consulates, and other facilities, are also considered noncombatant targets.

Although only acts of violence against noncombatant targets are counted as terrorism incidents, an incident that also resulted in the death of combatant victims includes a count of these victims as well. In an incident where combatants are the targets of the event, noncombatants who are incidentally harmed are designated "collateral" and the incident is excluded from the posted data set. For example, if terrorists attack a military base in Iraq and wound one civilian bystander, that victim is deemed to be collateral, and the incident is not counted.

- However, there is an exception. If an attack, even if it appeared to be directed against a combatant target, includes the deliberate harming of civilian bystanders in the immediate vicinity of the attack, the attack is designated a terrorist incident. For example, if assailants strike a military checkpoint, and they flee the scene gunning down civilian travelers approaching the checkpoint, this attack would be considered an incident.

Terrorist-on-terrorist violence is not considered a terrorist incident, nor is environmental related terrorism. Terrorists must initiate and execute an attack for it to be designated as a terrorist incident; foiled attacks are not considered an incident.

Examples of 2006 Events Judged Not To Be a Terror Incident

- In Nepal on 5 February, authorities defused several bombs on a college campus that were planted by suspected Maoists. Because the attack was thwarted, it is not recorded as an incident.
- In Turkey on 28 March, funerals for members of the Kurdistan Workers' Party were beset by violence that killed nine and wounded 250 other civilians. Mob violence was judged to be the cause behind the event and it was not recorded as an incident.
- In Israel on 3 February, Hizballah fired mortar rounds at an Israeli Army base, wounding a soldier. Because the soldier is in "combatant' status, and the base is a military facility, the shelling was not recorded as a terrorism incident.

Unless a possible political motivation can be determined from open-source reporting, violent acts that result in noncombatant victims being found in the public domain, such as parks, rivers, and riverbanks, are not designated as terrorist incidents.

What Is "Politically Motivated Violence?"

NCTC has established criteria to distinguish politically motivated, terrorism related violence from other forms of violence. Any life threatening attack or kidnapping is considered a terrorist incident if it is conducted by a "Foreign Terrorist Organization" or group on the list of "Other Organizations of Concern" established by the Department of State in its annual report on terrorism. Similarly, any serious attack by any organization or individual against a government or diplomatic official or facility is deemed politically motivated and is therefore considered terrorism. In contrast, any terrorist organization's actions that are primarily intended to enable future terrorist attacks, such as a bank robbery to raise money, are not considered incidents unless the perpetrators deliberately harm civilian bystanders in the immediate vicinity of the attack.

Determining the "politically motivated" nexus of an incident is highly subjective in many instances, especially when little information is available. If information about an attack is insufficient—for example, key elements such as perpetrators and victims are unknown—to determine a nexus to political violence, the attack is not recorded as an incident. For example, if deceased victims are found anywhere, such as floating in a river, and details about the circumstances and motives regarding the deaths are unknown, an incident is not recorded—the deaths could be a result of criminal or other nonterrorism motives such as rage or hate related violence.

In the case of Iraq, open-source information about attacks is often insufficient to clearly distinguish terrorism from the numerous other forms of nonterrorism-related violence. The key distinction between terrorism and others forms of violence is that noncombatants are victimized for what at least appear to be politically motivated purposes. For a violent act to be designated as a terrorist incident, enough information must be available to establish these two key elements: that the victims appear to be noncombatants, and that they are targeted primarily for what appears to be politically motivated reasons.

- An attack against noncombatants that reflects terrorist methods and occurs in areas where subnational groups or clandestine agents are active participants in an insurgency or stirring serious political instability, is likely to be designated a terrorist attack if information is sufficient to establish a possible political motive.

Determining "politically motivated" violence is a particularly difficult distinction to draw in some regions. For example, determining an incident of terrorism can be particularly problematic for attacks in Africa, where various forms of ethnic and tribal violence occur in areas that are relatively ungoverned by the state. Tribal groups in unstable areas such as these often act as governing bodies in the absence of effective central government control and thus their actions in many instances are politically motivated. For the purposes of counting terrorist incidents, NCTC distinguishes two general cases.

- When armed personnel of tribal groups come into direct conflict with one another and noncombatants become victims of collateral damage, the violence is similar to war-like circumstances and is not considered an incident of terrorism.
- In contrast, when an armed group recklessly targets and harms local populations, such as unarmed villagers, these attacks are considered terrorism against noncombatants.

An Academic's Perspective of Statistical Data

"In this short note, which was invited by NCTC, I highlight some of the challenges encountered in producing credible data on terrorist incidents. The WITS database strikes me as a particularly useful resource to use to evaluate trends in terrorist activity, to infer patterns in terrorists' methods in order to take the best possible precautions, and to test hypotheses concerning the cause of terrorism. With these applications in mind, there are three areas in which the WITS data deserve particular attention: Definition, measurement, and significance. The definition is missing two important pieces, whether or not an attack is international or domestic, and political violence 'usually intended to influence an audience.' Measurement of the error rate in the WITS data is important to understand. Statistical techniques used by other government statistical agencies could be adopted to measure the rate of error, comprehensiveness, and consistency of the WITS data. These measures will facilitate use of the WITS data by researchers and highlight areas where the data are weak. Providing measures of significance of events (e.g., a terrorist Richter scale running from 1 to 5) and coder confidence would be particularly useful. The collection and provision of data like the WITS is a quintessential public good, and NCTC is the most appropriate government agency to collect such data."

Alan B. Krueger, Princeton University

April 11, 2007 (Entire letter is presented in the appendix.)

General Observations of Worldwide Incidents of Terror

Approximately 14,000 terrorist attacks occurred in various countries during 2006, resulting in over 20,000 deaths. As compared to 2005, terrorist incidents in 2006 rose by 3,000, a 25 percent increase, while deaths rose by 5,800, a 40 percent increase. As was the case in 2005, by far the largest number of reported terrorist incidents and related deaths during 2006 occurred in the Near East and South Asia. These two regions also were the locations for 90 percent of the nearly 300 high-casualty attacks that killed 10 or more people—only five high-casualty attacks occurred in Europe-Eurasia, East Asia-Pacific, and the Western Hemisphere.

- Of the 14,000 reported attacks, 45 percent—about 6600—occurred in Iraq where approximately 13,000 fatalities—65 percent of the worldwide total—were reported for 2006.
- Violence against noncombatants in East and sub-Saharan Africa, particularly related to attacks associated with turmoil in or near Sudan and Nigeria, rose 64 percent in 2006, rising to 422 from the approximately 256 attacks reported for 2005.
- The approximately 750 attacks in Afghanistan during 2006 are 50 percent more than the nearly 500 attacks reported for 2005 as fighting intensified during the past year.
- The number of reported incidents in 2006 fell for Europe and Eurasia by 15 percent from those in 2005, for South Asia, by 10 percent, and for the Western Hemisphere, by 5 percent. No high-casualty attacks occurred in Western Europe, and only one occurred in Southeast Asia, in the southern Philippines. In Indonesia, there were no high-casualty attacks and 95 percent fewer victims of terror in 2006, as compared with 2005, which is likely attributable to a more robust regional counterterrorism effort.

The number injured during terrorist incidents rose substantially in 2006, as compared with the previous year, by 54 percent, with most of the rise stemming from a doubling of the reported number of injuries in Iraq since 2005. Although kidnappings in Iraq tripled in 2006, kidnappings overall declined by more than 50 percent in 2006 because of a steep drop of approximately 22,000 kidnappings in Nepal where peace discussions during the year apparently curtailed hostage taking.

Attackers

The perpetrators of more than 9,000 terrorist attacks in 2006 could not be determined from open-source information. Of the remaining incidents, as many as 290 various subnational groups—many of them well-known foreign terrorist organizations such as AQI—or clandestine agents were connected to an attack in various ways, including as a claimant, as the accused, or as the possible or probable perpetrator. In most instances, open-source reporting contains little confirmed or corroborating information that identifies the organizations or individuals responsible for a terrorist attack. In many reports, attackers are alleged to be tied to local or well-known terrorist groups but there is little subsequent reporting that verifies these connections. Moreover, pinpointing attackers becomes even more difficult as extremist groups splinter or merge with others, make false claims, or deny allegations.

- According to open-source reports, Sunni terrorist groups, more than any other subnational group, claimed that they conducted the largest number of incidents with the highest casualty totals.
- Sunni terrorist groups in various countries carried out about the same number of high fatality attacks in 2006, as compared with those in 2005, but with deadlier results, and they were involved in more kidnappings than these extremists reportedly carried out in 2005.

Although no terrorist attack occurred in 2006 that approached the sophistication of planning and preparations that were characteristic of the 9/11 attacks, open-source reporting alleges that al-Qa'ida leaders played an important role in steering terrorists in the United Kingdom who were in August plotting to blow up multiple US-bound commercial planes. Reporting points to a steadfast al-Qa'ida that is planning attacks in northwest Pakistan, and was able to expand its propaganda campaign in 2006 to invigorate supporters, win converts, and gain recruits while its al-Qa'ida in Iraq associates and other linked groups carried out several successful attacks.

- Al-Qa'ida in the Arabian Peninsula conducted the first-ever terrorist attack against a Saudi Arabia oil facility at the major oil processing plant at Abqaiq on 24 February 2006. Security forces, which suffered a few casualties, prevented the attackers from damaging processing capabilities.
- According to open-sources, the al-Qa'ida senior leadership approved the merger with the Salafist Group for Preaching and Combat (GSPC), which conducted its first attack against a US target at La Trappe, Algeria on 10 December. The GSPC remotely detonated a bomb that struck a bus and wounded one of the US passengers who worked for a US company, and the attackers subsequently used smalls arms to fire bullets at the bus, killing or wounding 9 non-US civilians.

Types of Attacks

As in 2005, most attacks in 2006 were perpetrated by terrorists applying conventional fighting methods that included using bombs and weapons, such as small arms. However, technology continues to empower terrorists and effective methods of attack continue to be developed by them to offset countermeasures. Terrorists continued their practice of coordinated attacks that included secondary attacks on first responders at attack sites, and they uniquely configured weapons and other materials to create improvised explosive devices (IEDs).

- While bombing incidents increased by 30 percent from those in 2005, the death tolls in these incidents during 2006 rose by 39 percent and injuries by 45 percent. The use of suicide bombing attacks overall fell 12 percent, most notably in the use of suicide car bombers. However, suicide bombers operating outside of vehicles increased by 25 percent, and the ability of these attackers to penetrate large concentrations of people and then detonate their explosives probably accounted for the increase in lethality of bombings in 2006.
- A new CBRN terrorist attack method in Iraq emerged in 2006. According to an Iraqi Interior Ministry explosive expert, a large vehicle-borne IED (VBIED) attack that included chemicals in Sadr City on 23 November signaled a dangerous strategic shift in tactics for 2007 that features the use of chemical weapons.

Use of VBIEDs in Iraq Against Noncombatants

Analysis of open source reporting shows that in incidents worldwide, terrorist employment of VBIEDs rose in 2006, although the use of VBIEDs in suicide attacks fell by 22 percent. In Iraq, suicide VBIED attacks declined overall, by 36 percent, in 2006 although during the last half of the year they returned to the level that was reached in 2005. The use of vehicles to deliver explosives occurred most often in Iraq where 566 VBIED attacks occurred, which represented 89 percent of these types of attacks carried out by terrorists in 2006.

Assailants continued to choose targets that will yield the greatest number of casualties, damage, and fear. In 2006, public places, such as markets and shopping centers, were targeted most often in VBIED attacks because they have a high population density.

- Of the total casualties caused by VBIED attacks in 2006, 94 percent of these occurred in Iraq.
- In one major incident, 91 civilians were killed, 121 others wounded in a triple VBIED attack on a market in Baghdad, Iraq.

Victims and Targets of Attacks

As in 2005, Muslims in 2006 again bore a substantial share of the victims of terrorist attacks.

- Approximately 58,000 individuals worldwide were either killed or injured by terrorist attacks in 2006. On the basis of a combination of reporting and demographic analysis of the countries involved, well over 50 percent of the victims were Muslims, and most were victims of attacks in Iraq.

Open-source reporting identifies approximately 70 percent of the 58,000 killed or injured victims of terror as simply civilians, and, therefore, actual tallies of significant types of victims cannot be specifically determined. However, the reporting does yield some insights about the demographics of these victims.

- Government officials such as leaders, police, department personnel, and paramilitary personnel such as guards, were reported 20 percent more often to be the victims, rising from approximately 9,500 in 2005 to just over 11,200 in 2006. More specifically, police victims were reported more often, their total rising more than 20 percent, from over 6,500 in 2005 to over 8,200 in 2006.
- More killings of educators were reported in 2006—148 deaths were highlighted in 2006 reporting as compared with 96 in 2005. Reporting of student victims increased over 320 percent, to over 430 either killed or injured in attacks, and reports of teachers as victims also increased by over 45 percent, reaching 214 either killed or injured in attacks.
- Children were also reported more often as victims in 2006, up by more than 80 percent from 2005, with over 1,800 children either killed or injured in terrorist attacks.
- More attacks involving journalists were reported in 2006, an increased of 5 percent compared with 2005. However, attacks involving reporters in 2006 resulted in 20 percent more journalist deaths and injuries than incidents that were reported in 2005.

US Deaths Resulting From Terrorism in 2006

According to the Department of State, there were 28 US fatalities as a result of terrorist attacks in 2006. Incidents in Iraq took the lives of 22 individuals, and another three died from incidents in Afghanistan. Three incidents, one each in Israel, Pakistan, and Thailand, claimed the lives of the remaining three victims.

In addition to the human toll, over 19,000 facilities were struck or were the targets during terrorist attacks last year. For both 2005 and 2006, the most common types of properties damaged or destroyed during an incident were vehicles and residences, which were hit in about 27 and 12 percent of the incidents, respectively. The percentage of incidents that included other types of property damage or destruction, such as those associated with energy, transportation, education, government, and other enterprises, remains unchanged at single digit levels with a few notable exceptions.

- Approximately 350 mosques were targeted or struck during attacks in 2006, in most cases by Islamic extremists, representing over a threefold increase from 2005. The attack against the Shia Golden Dome Mosque in Iraq, attributed to al-Qa'ida in Iraq, triggered a watershed of escalating sectarian violence in Iraq.

- Fewer incidents involved civilian aircraft and airports, resulting in less damage to both in 2006.
- Electoral polling stations saw over an 80 percent drop in attacks by terrorists in 2006.

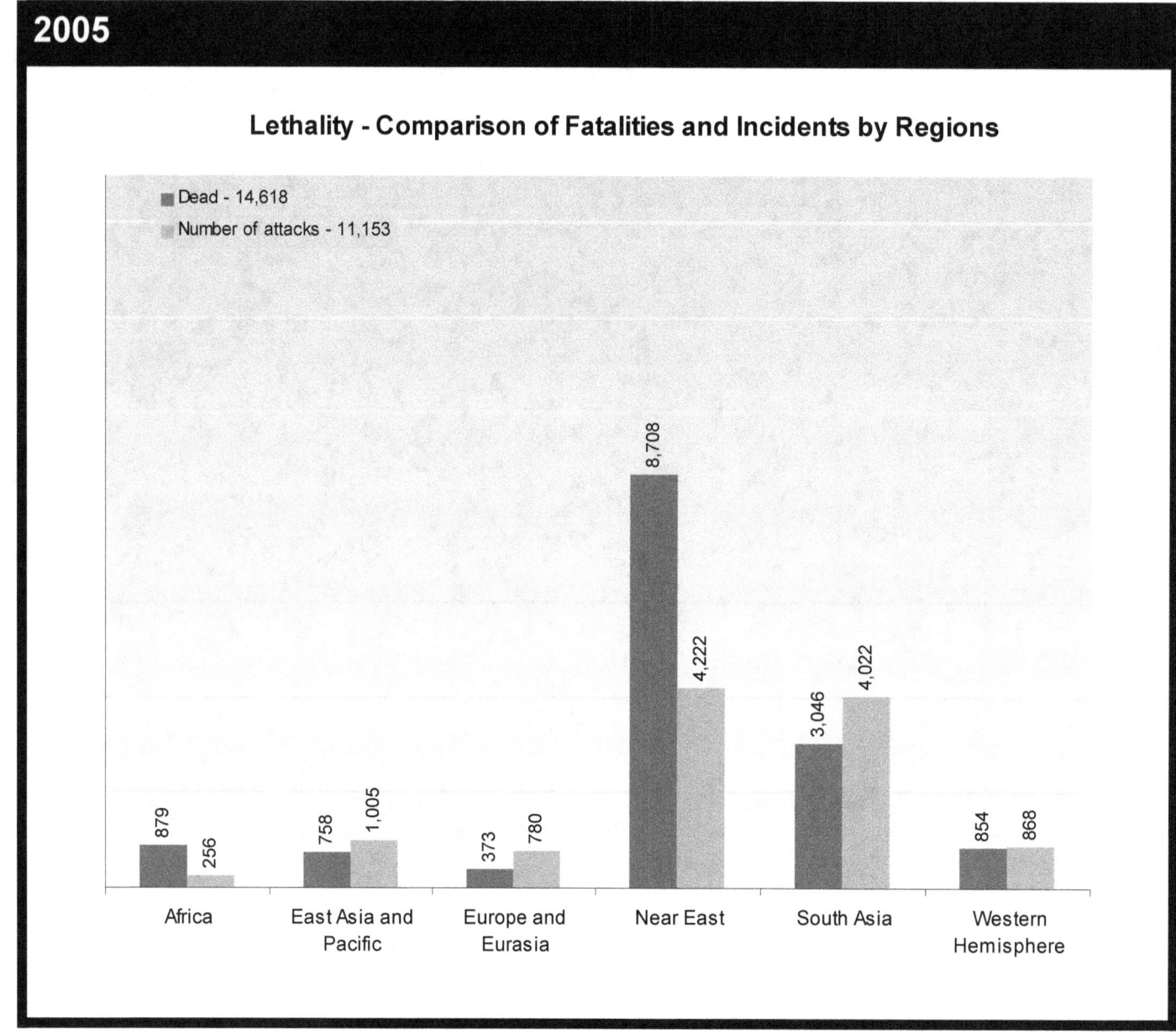

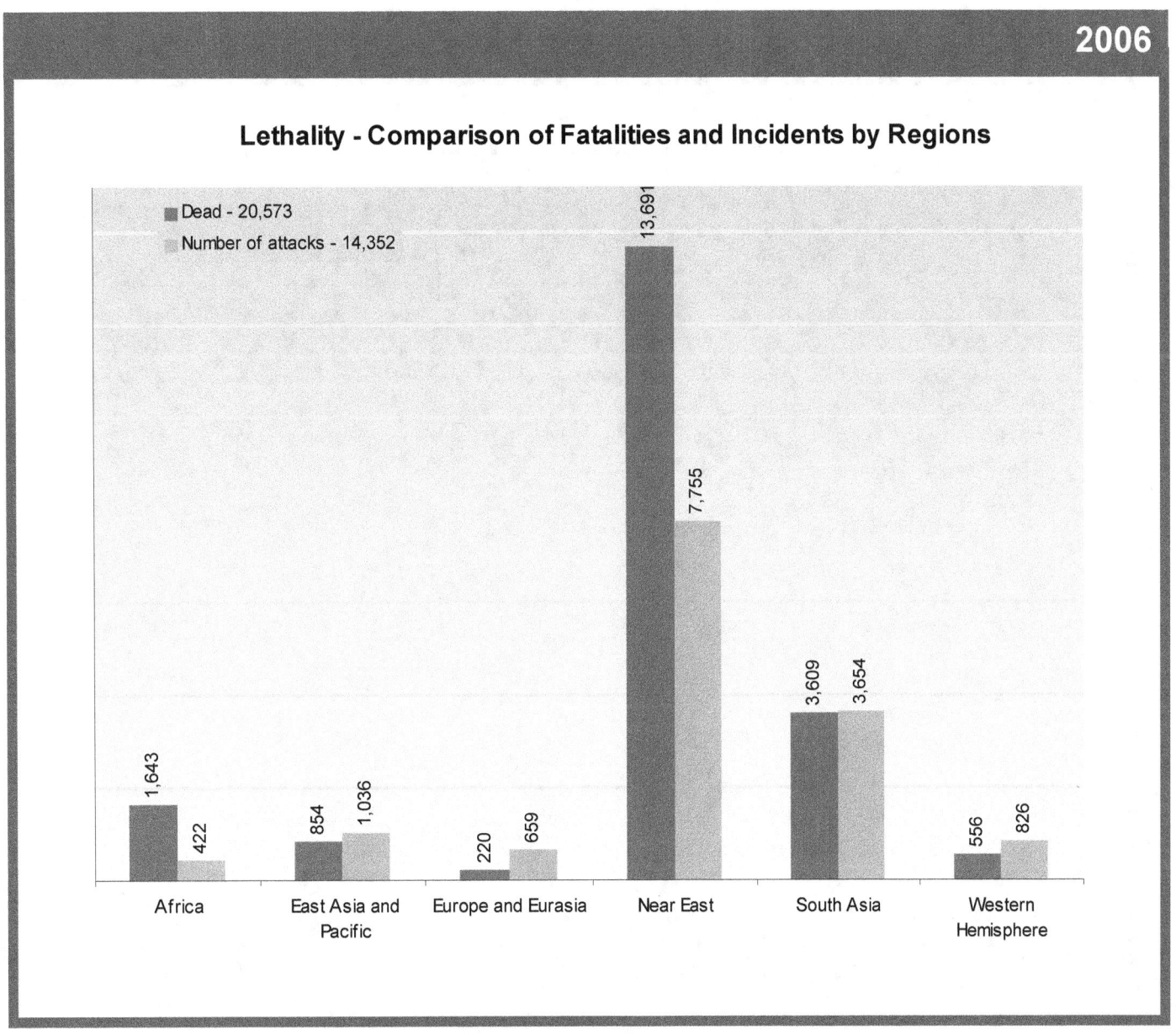

2005

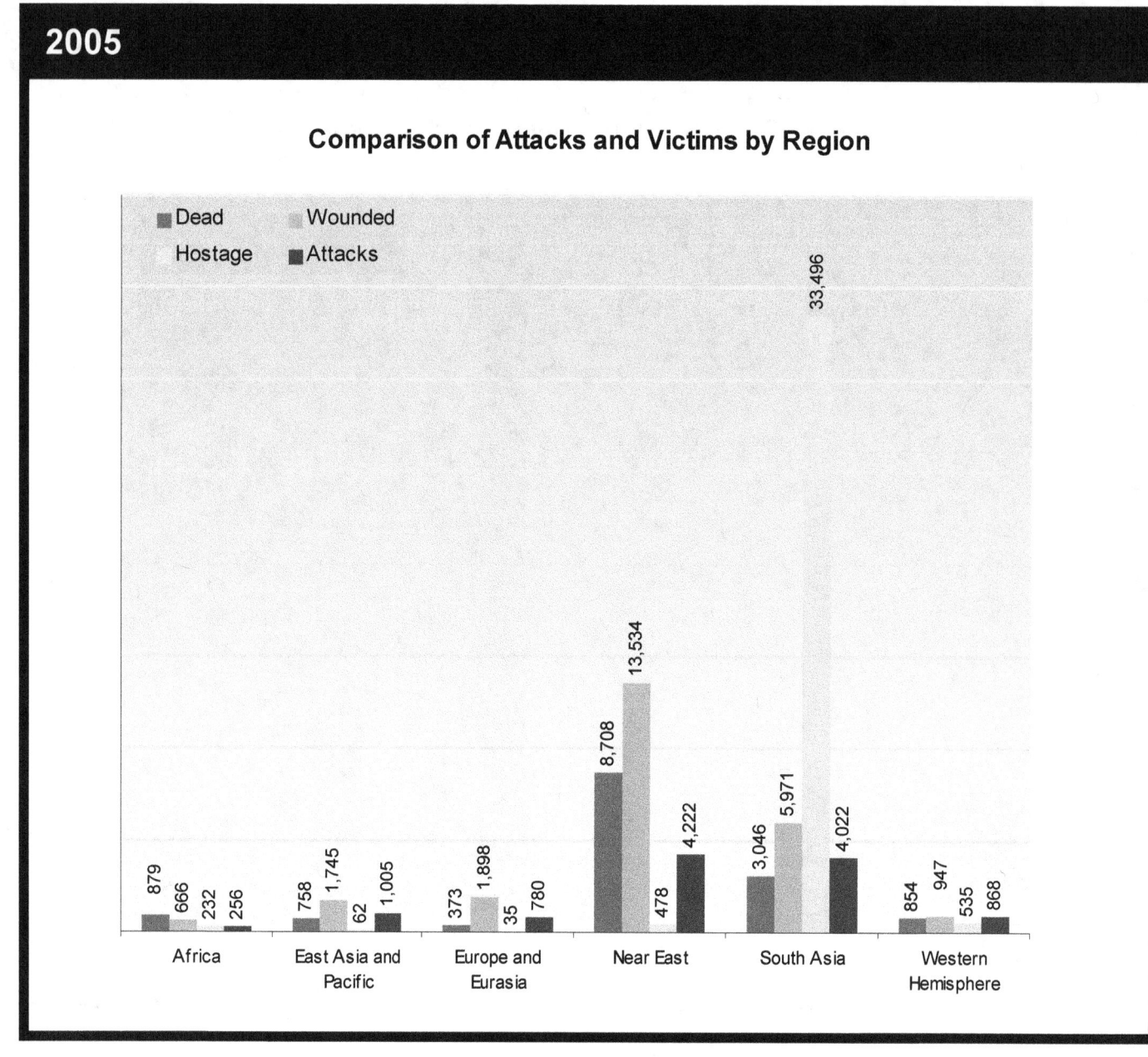

Comparison of Attacks and Victims by Region

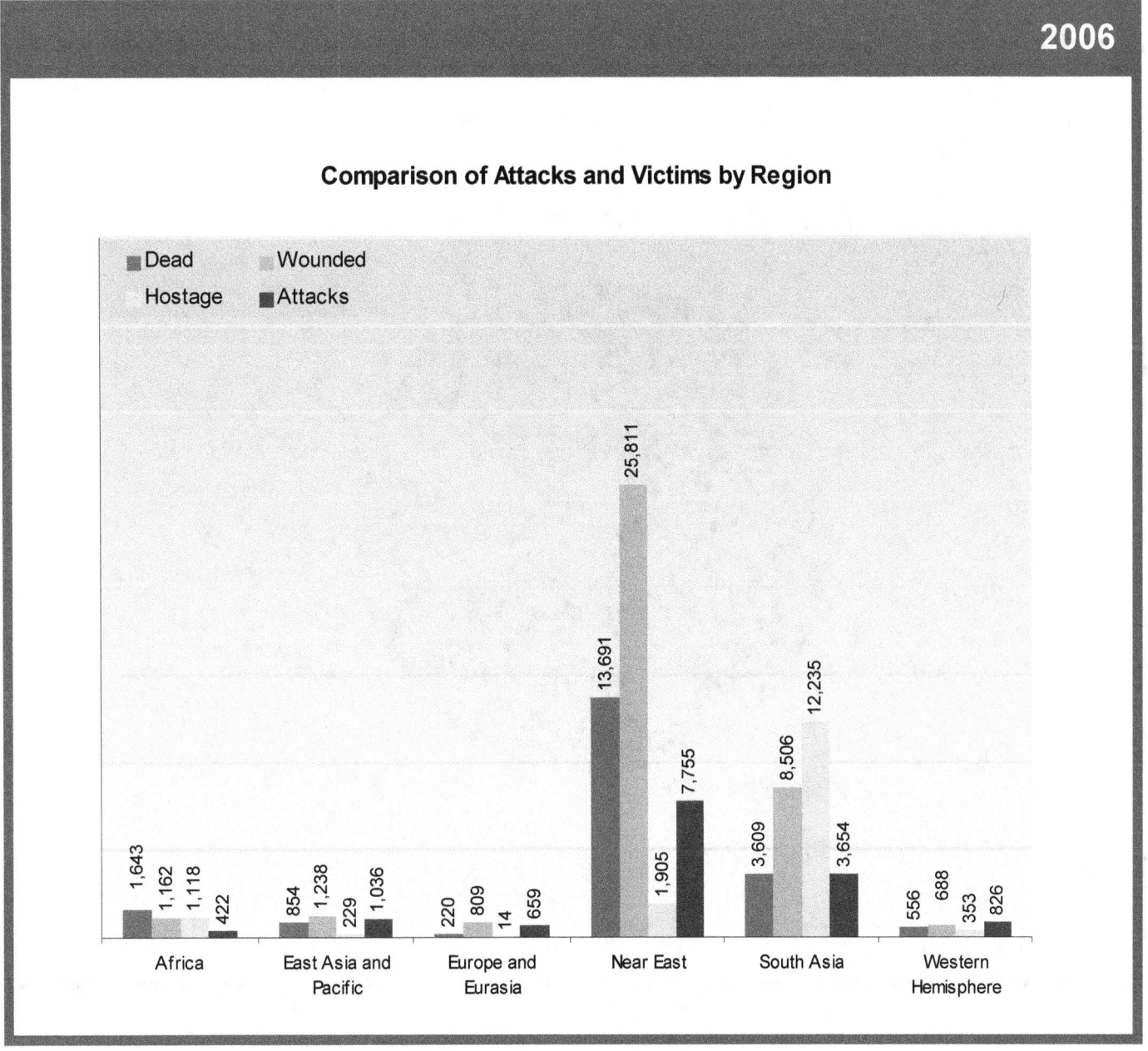

2005

Methods Used in Fatality Incidents

- Bombing - 37%
- Kidnapping - 5%
- Unknown - 4%
- Assault - 3%
- Arson/Firebombing - 2%
- Other - 0%
- Barricade/Hostage - 0%
- Armed Attack - 49%

14,618 Total Deaths in 2005

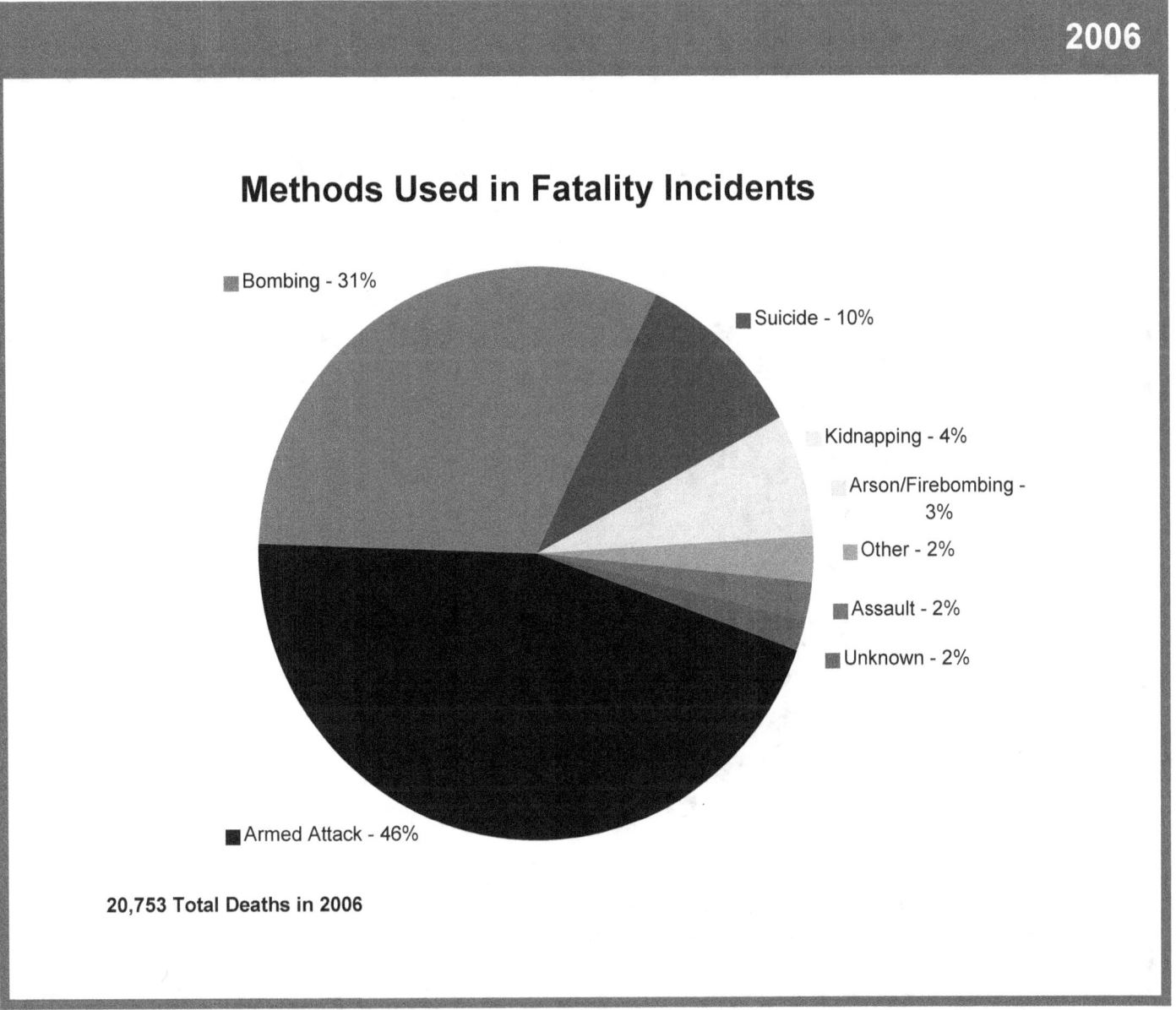

Methods Used in Fatality Incidents

- Bombing - 31%
- Suicide - 10%
- Kidnapping - 4%
- Arson/Firebombing - 3%
- Other - 2%
- Assault - 2%
- Unknown - 2%
- Armed Attack - 46%

20,753 Total Deaths in 2006

2005

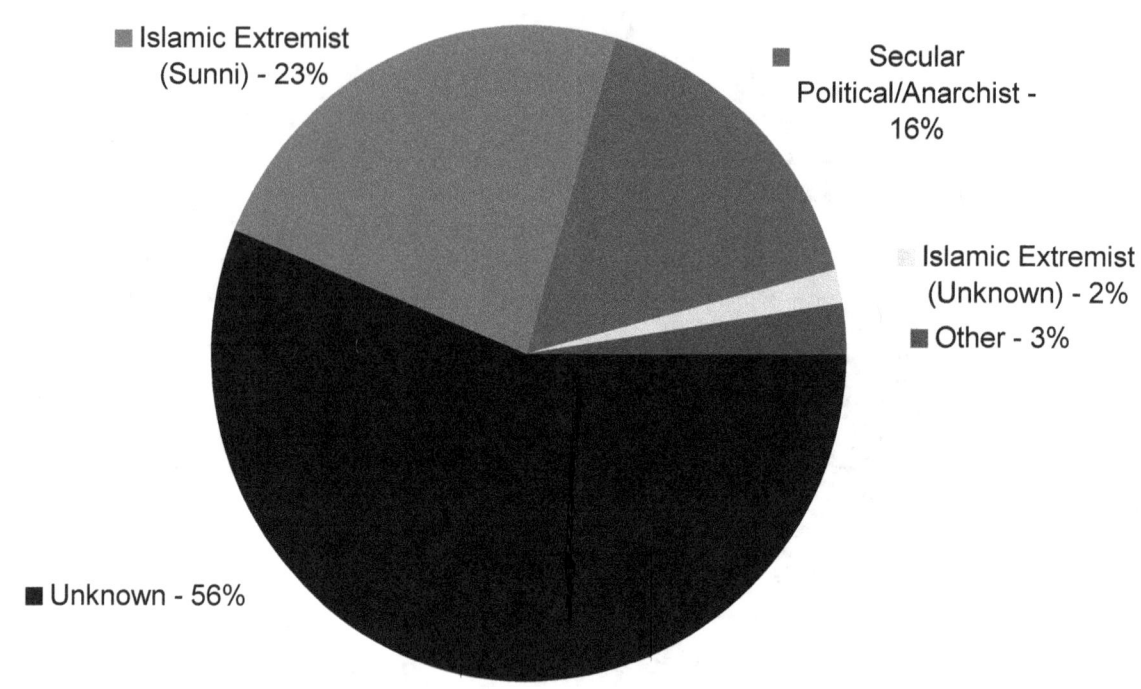

Fatalities by Perpetrator Category

14,618 Total Deaths in 2005
Some double counting when joint claims were made.
Categories include attacks either claimed or suspected

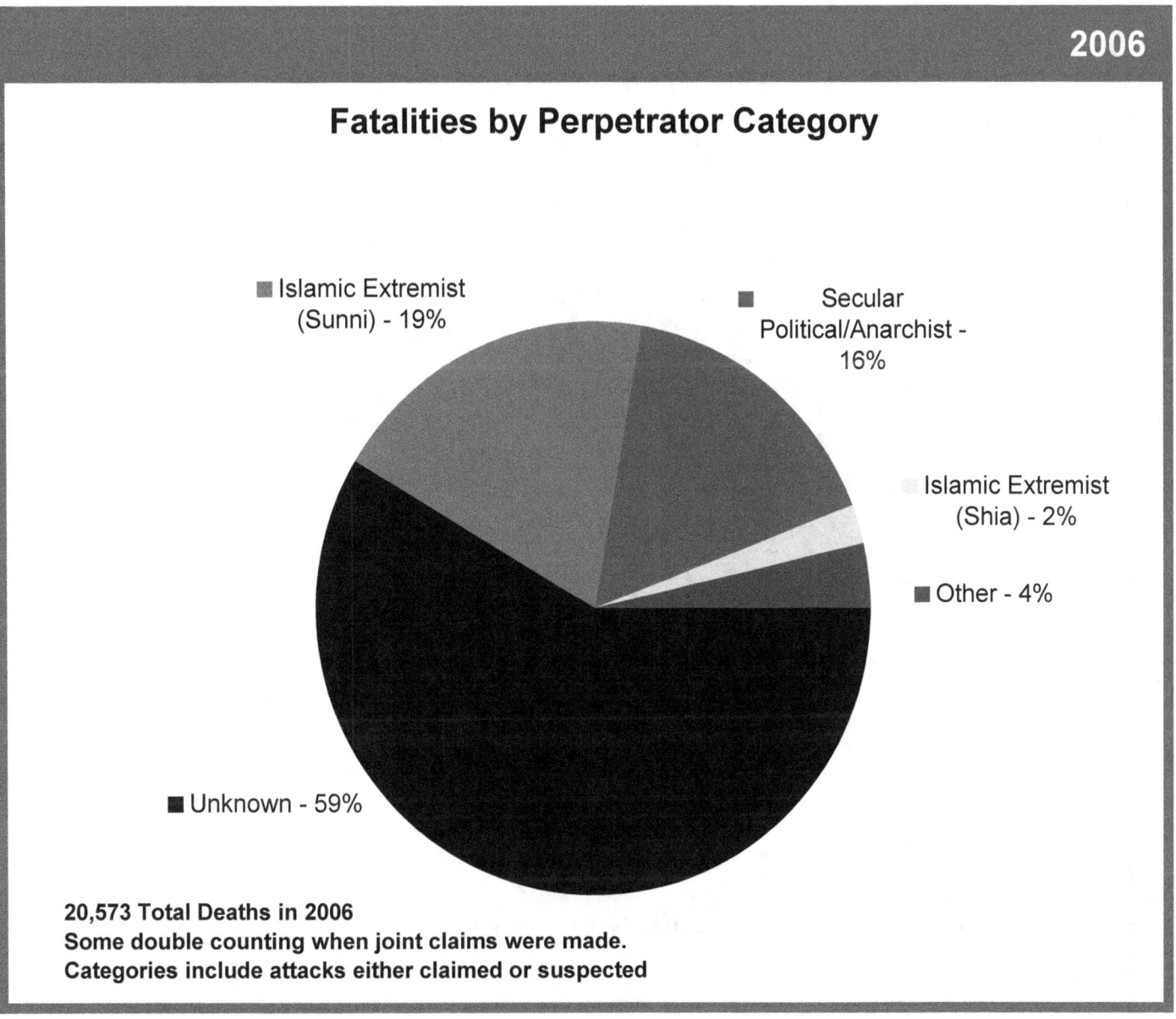

2005

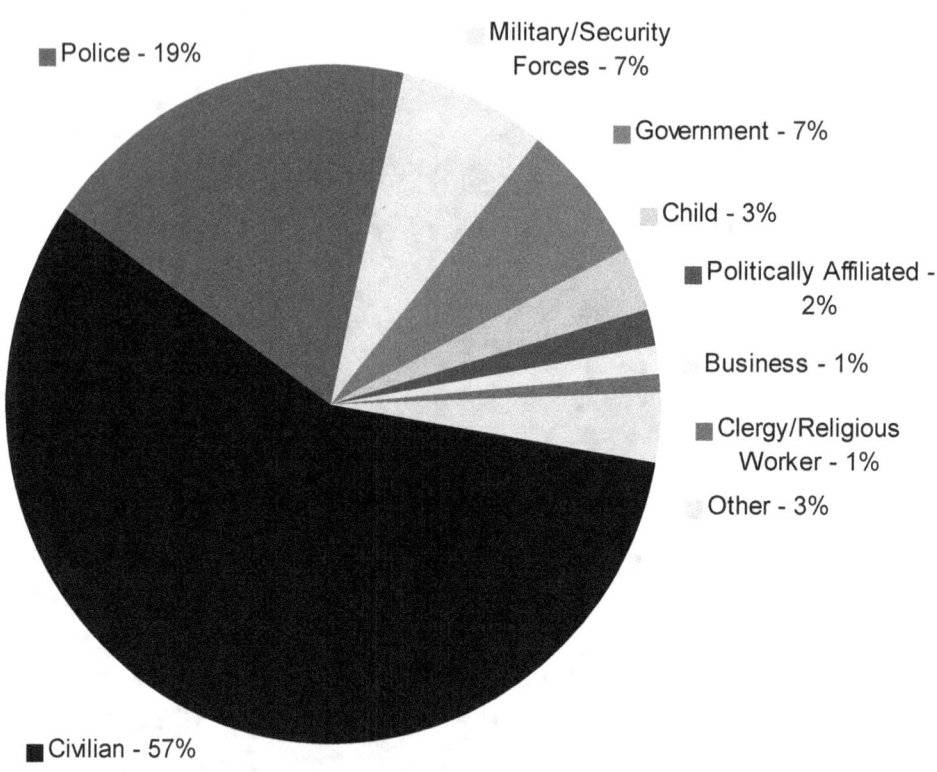

Fatalities by Victim Category

14,618 Total Deaths in 2005
Children were double counted, typically as civilians

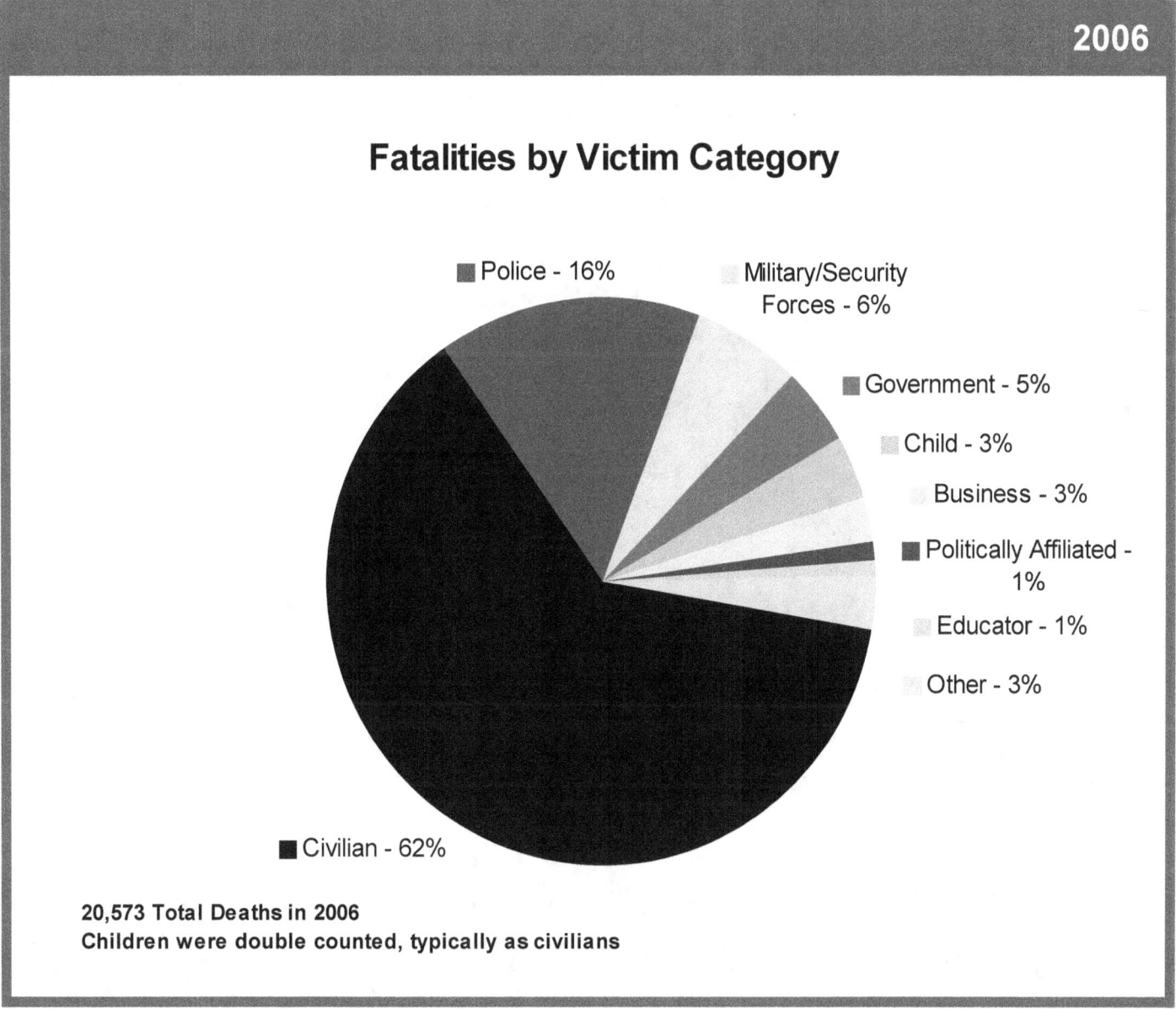

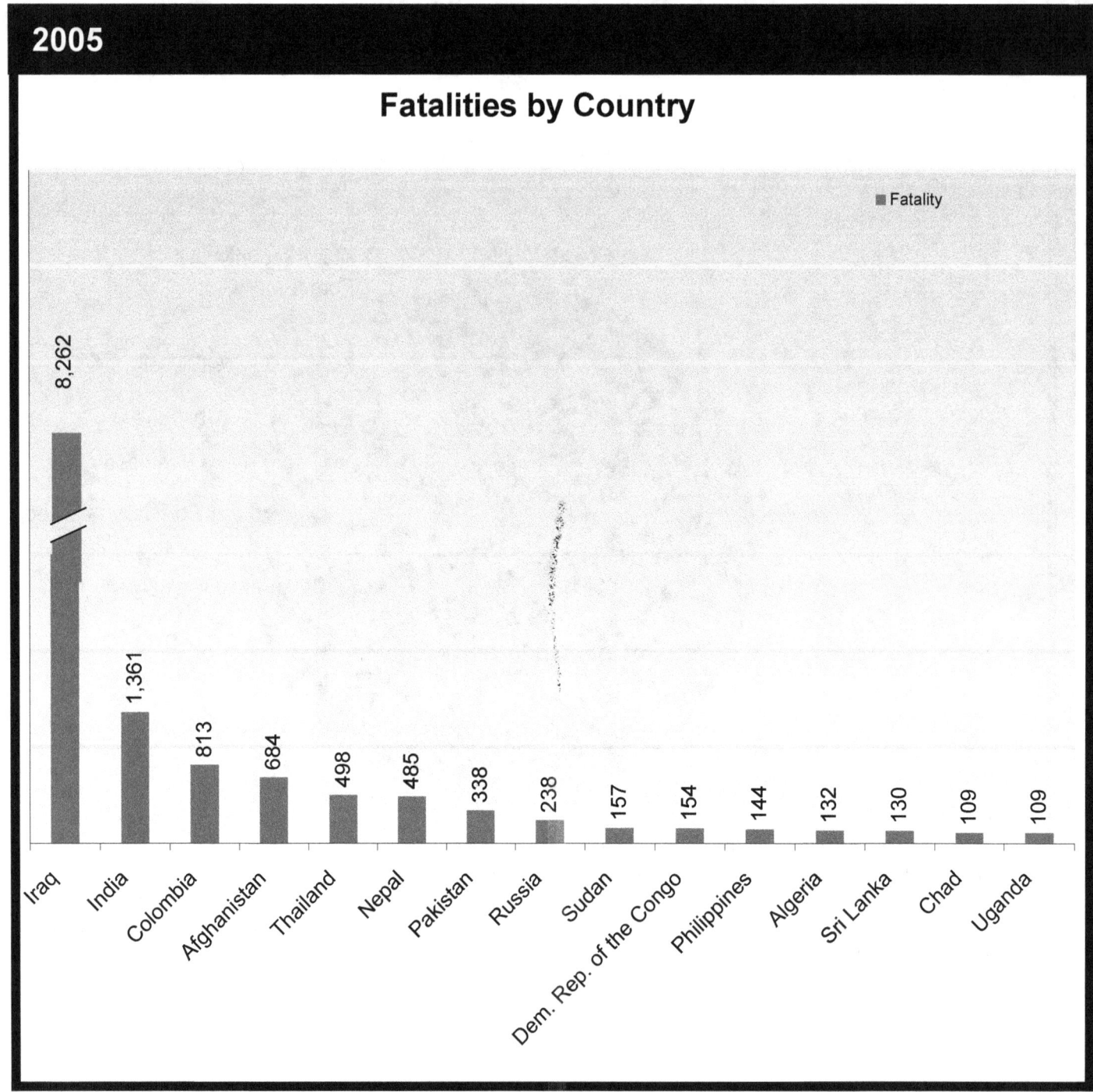

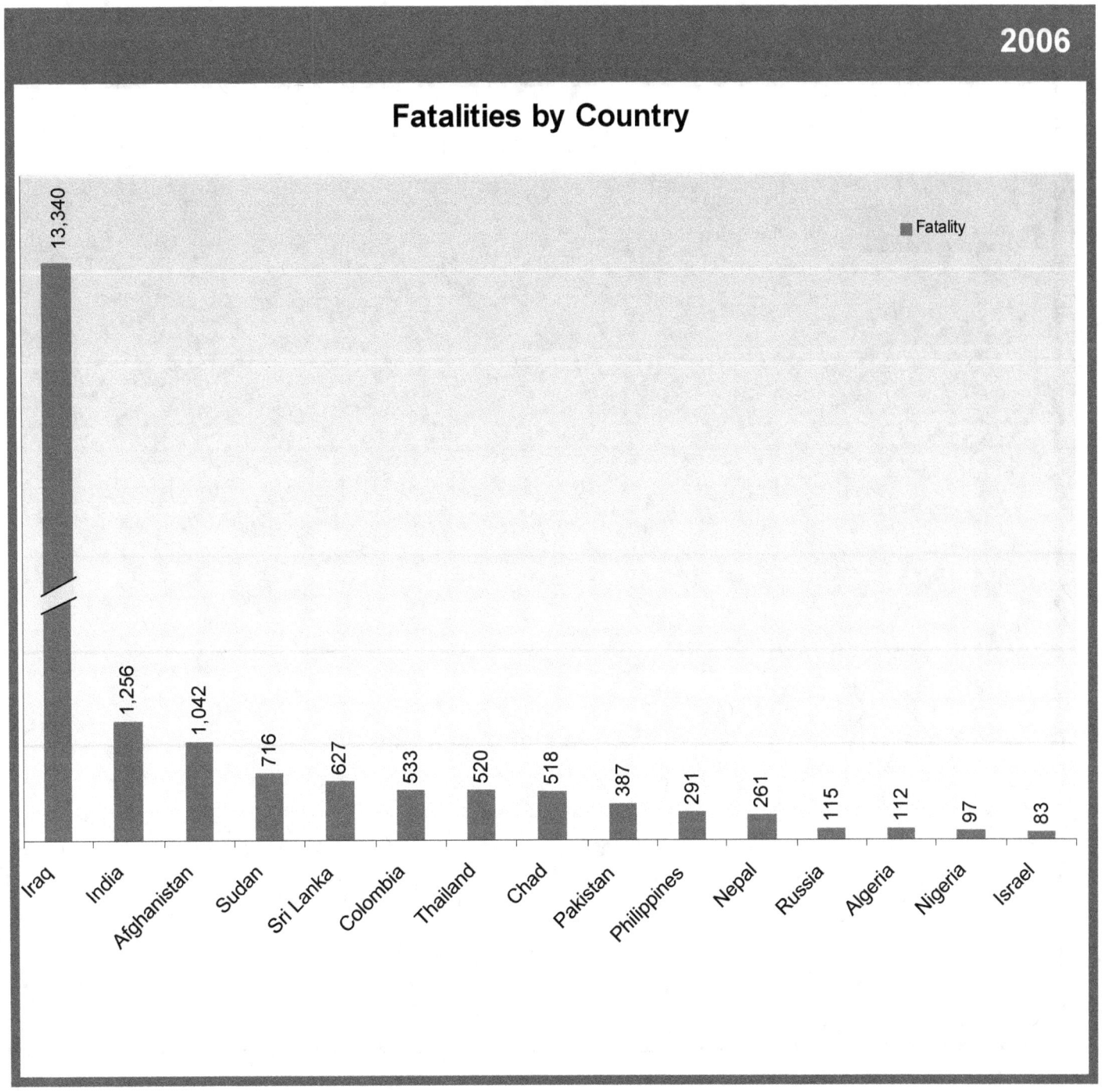

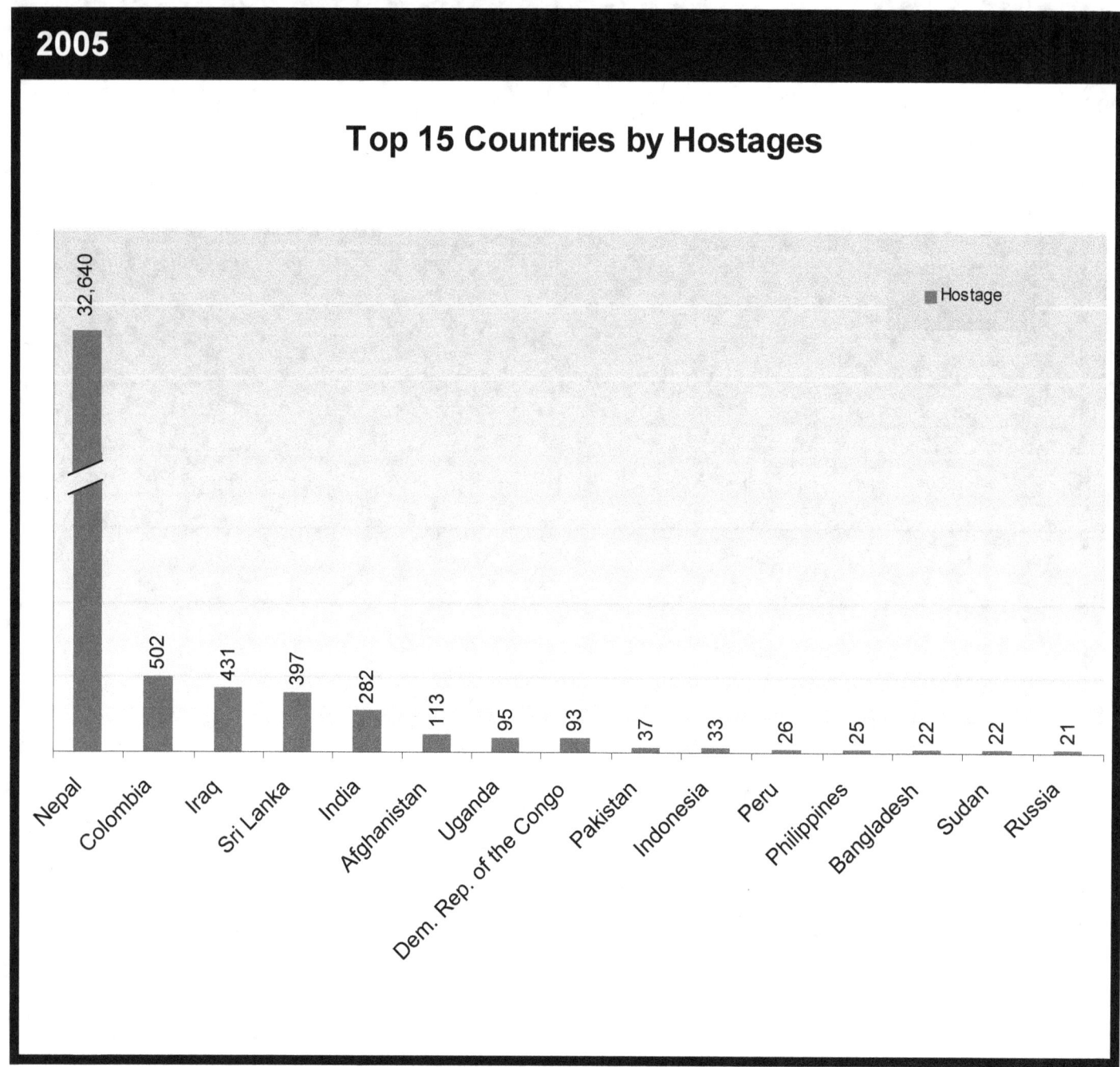

2005

Top 15 Countries by Hostages

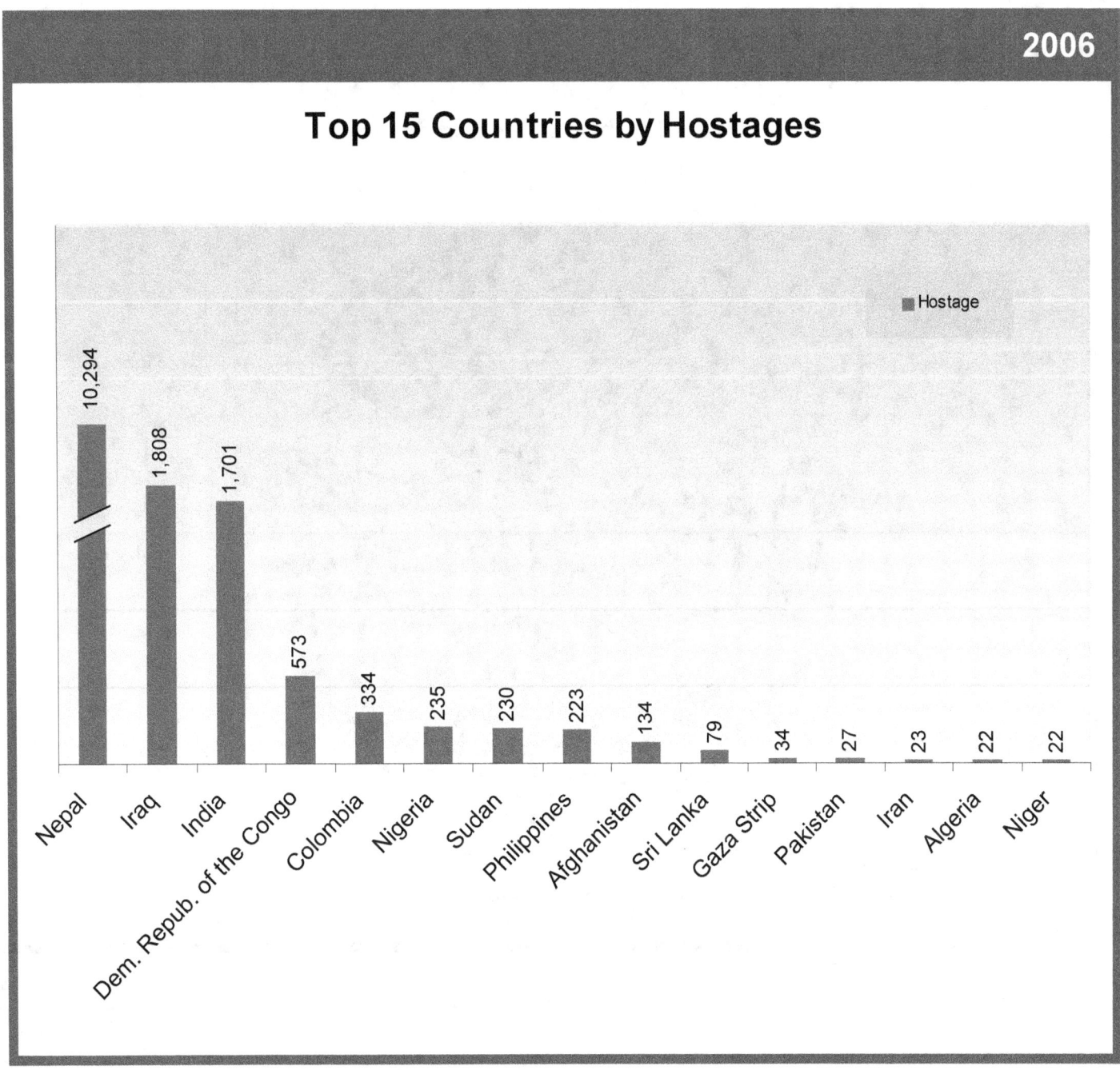

2005

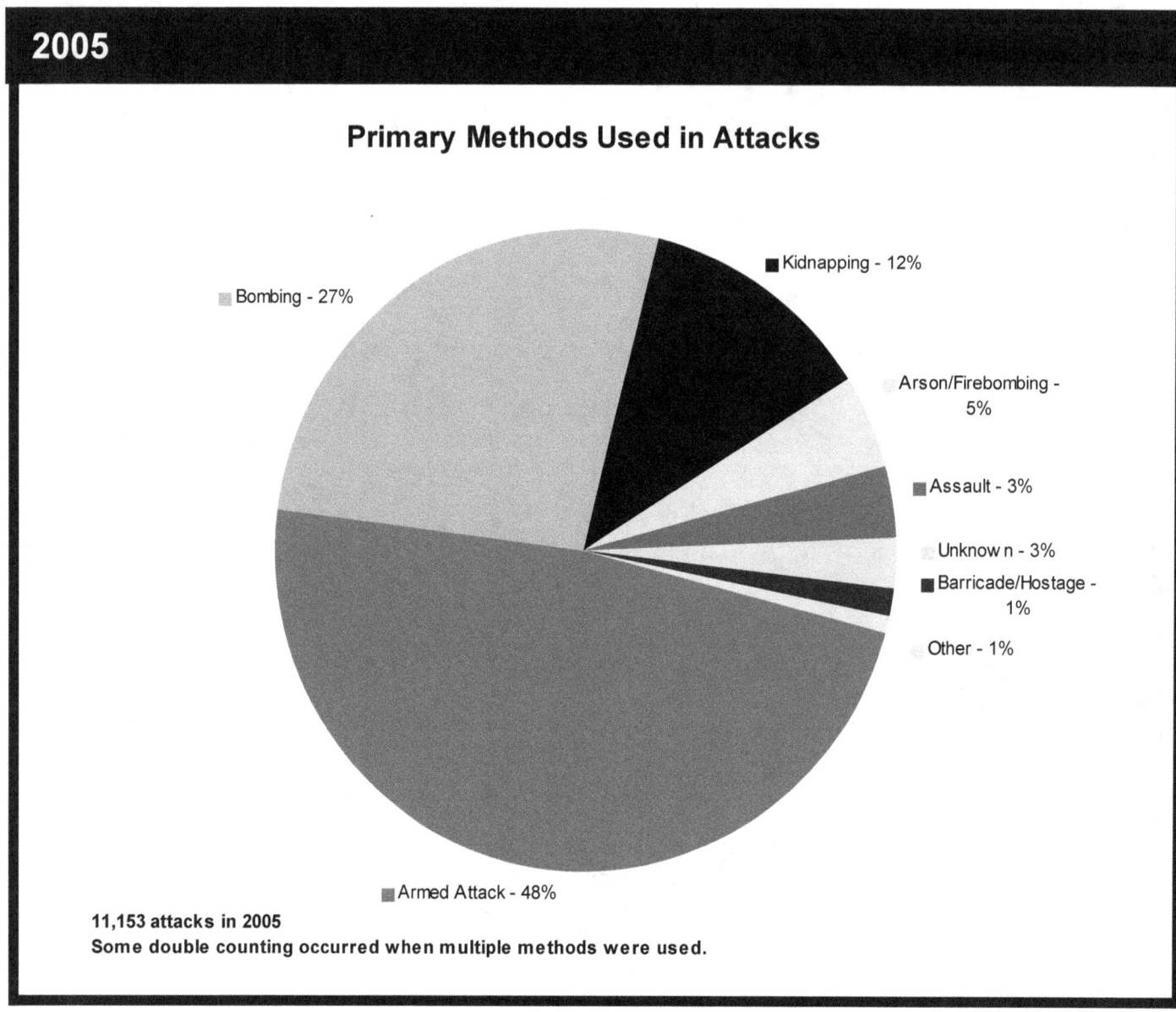

Primary Methods Used in Attacks

■ Kidnapping - 12%

Arson/Firebombing - 5%

■ Assault - 3%

Unknown - 3%

■ Barricade/Hostage - 1%

Other - 1%

■ Bombing - 27%

■ Armed Attack - 48%

11,153 attacks in 2005
Some double counting occurred when multiple methods were used.

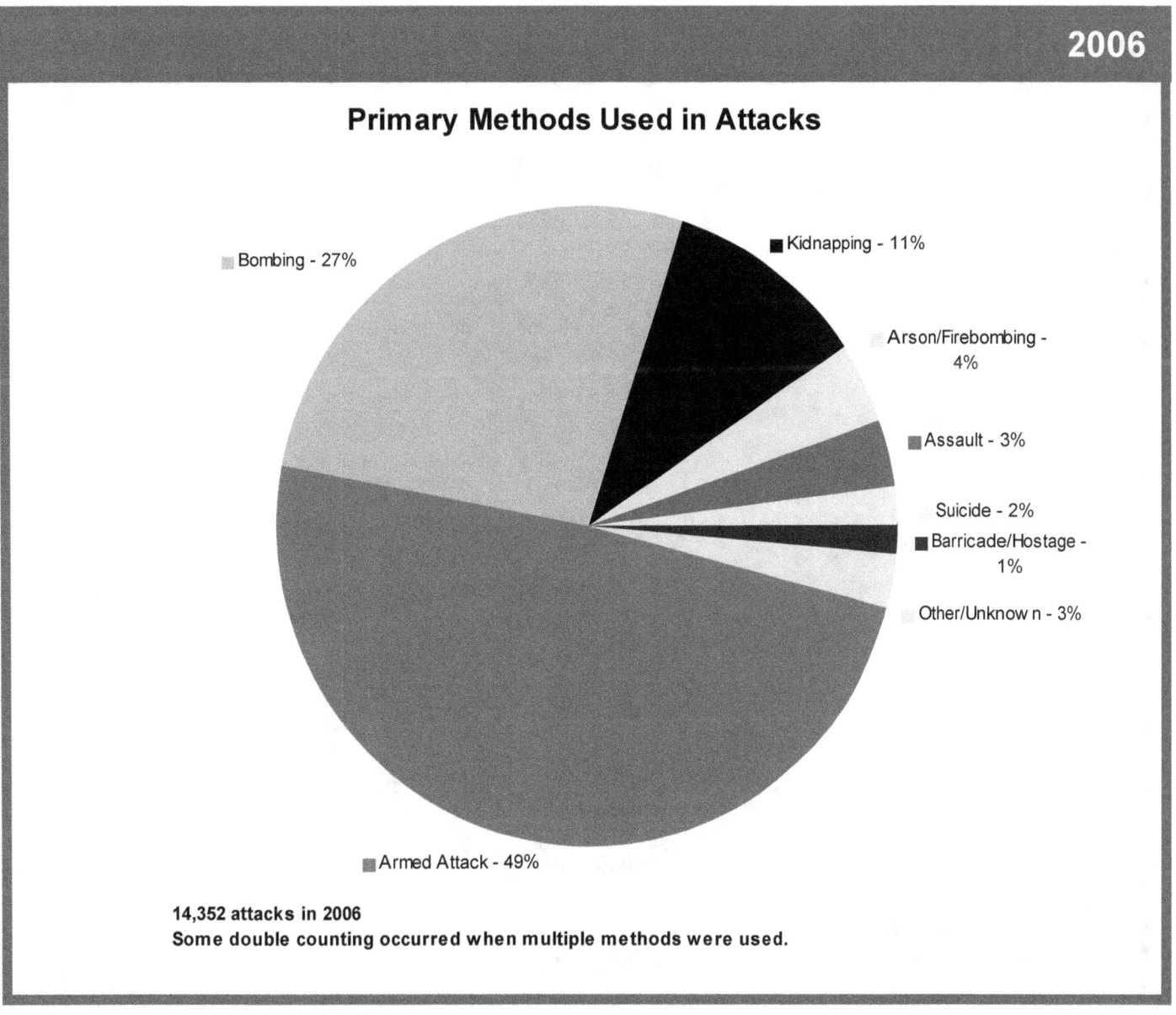

2005

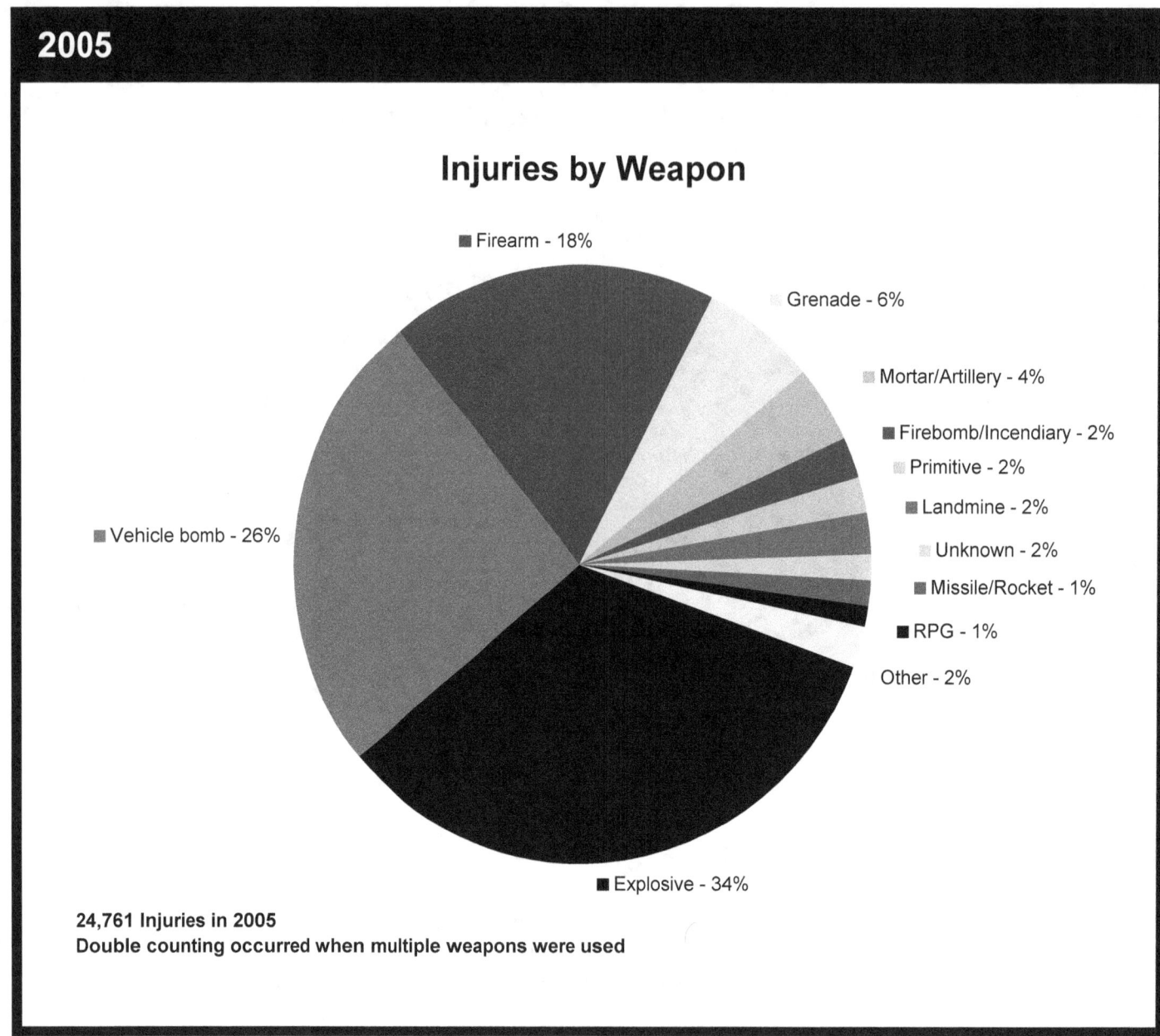

Injuries by Weapon

24,761 Injuries in 2005
Double counting occurred when multiple weapons were used

30

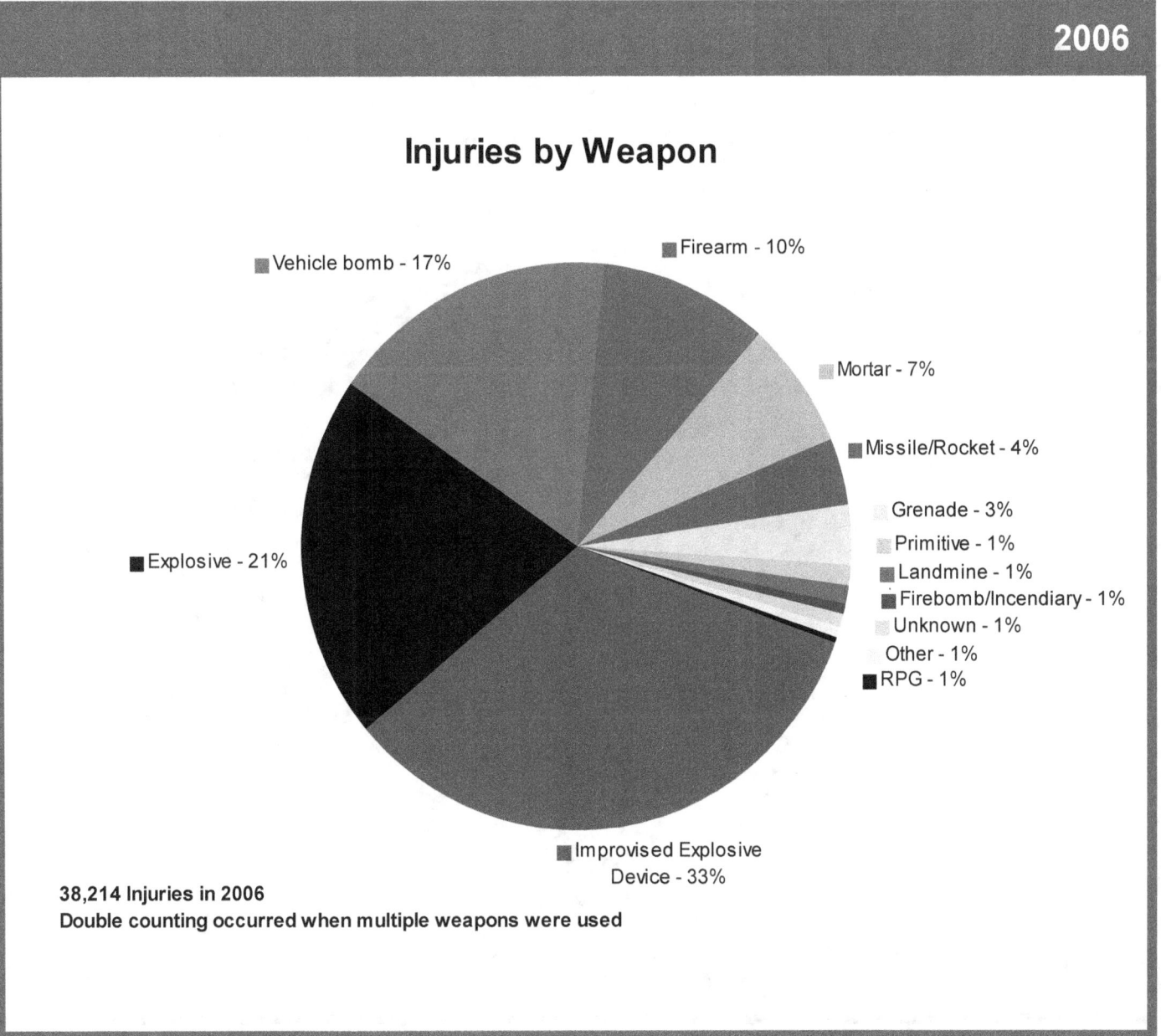

Injuries by Weapon

- Vehicle bomb - 17%
- Firearm - 10%
- Mortar - 7%
- Missile/Rocket - 4%
- Grenade - 3%
- Primitive - 1%
- Landmine - 1%
- Firebomb/Incendiary - 1%
- Unknown - 1%
- Other - 1%
- RPG - 1%
- Explosive - 21%
- Improvised Explosive Device - 33%

38,214 Injuries in 2006
Double counting occurred when multiple weapons were used

2006

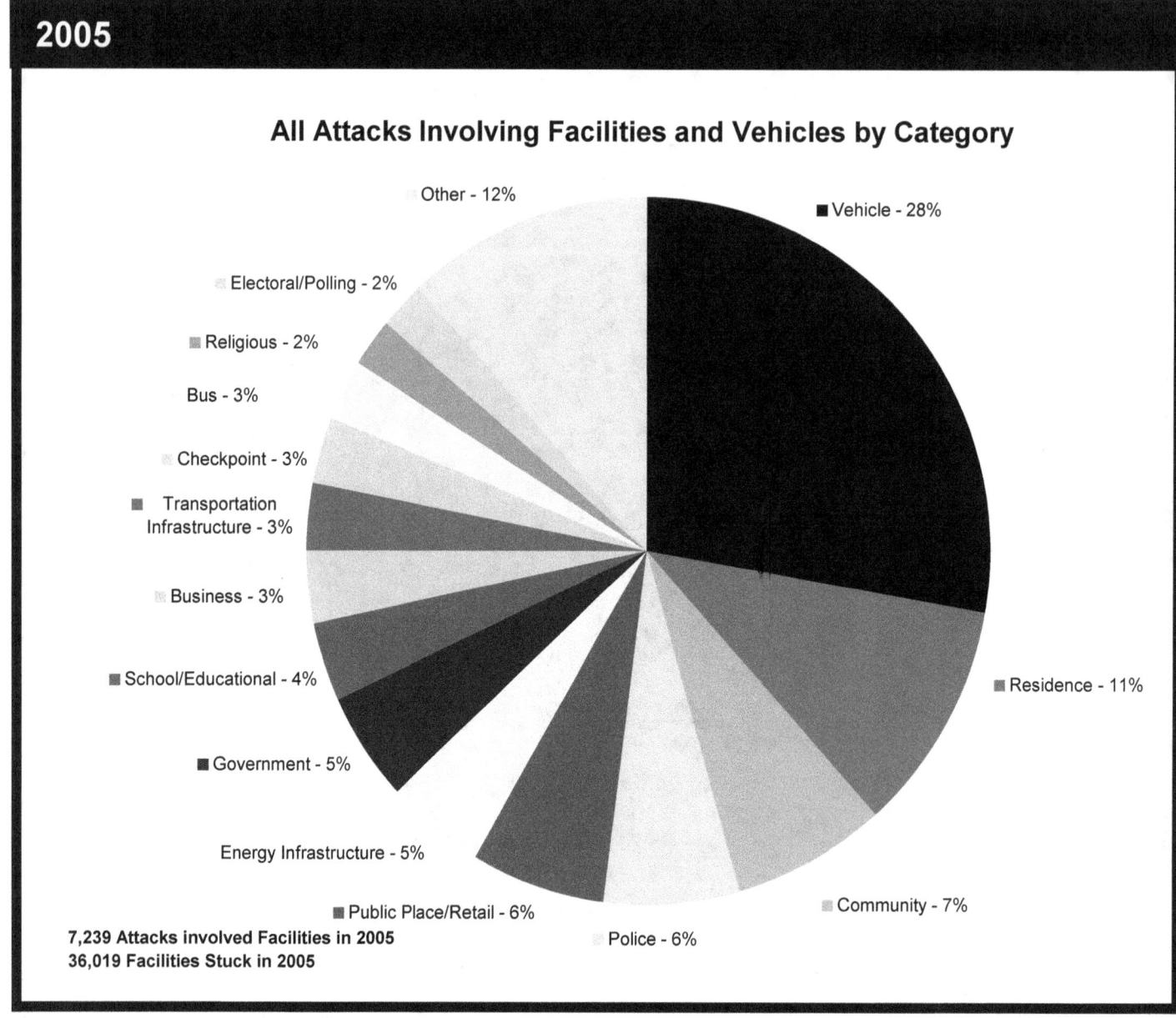

2006

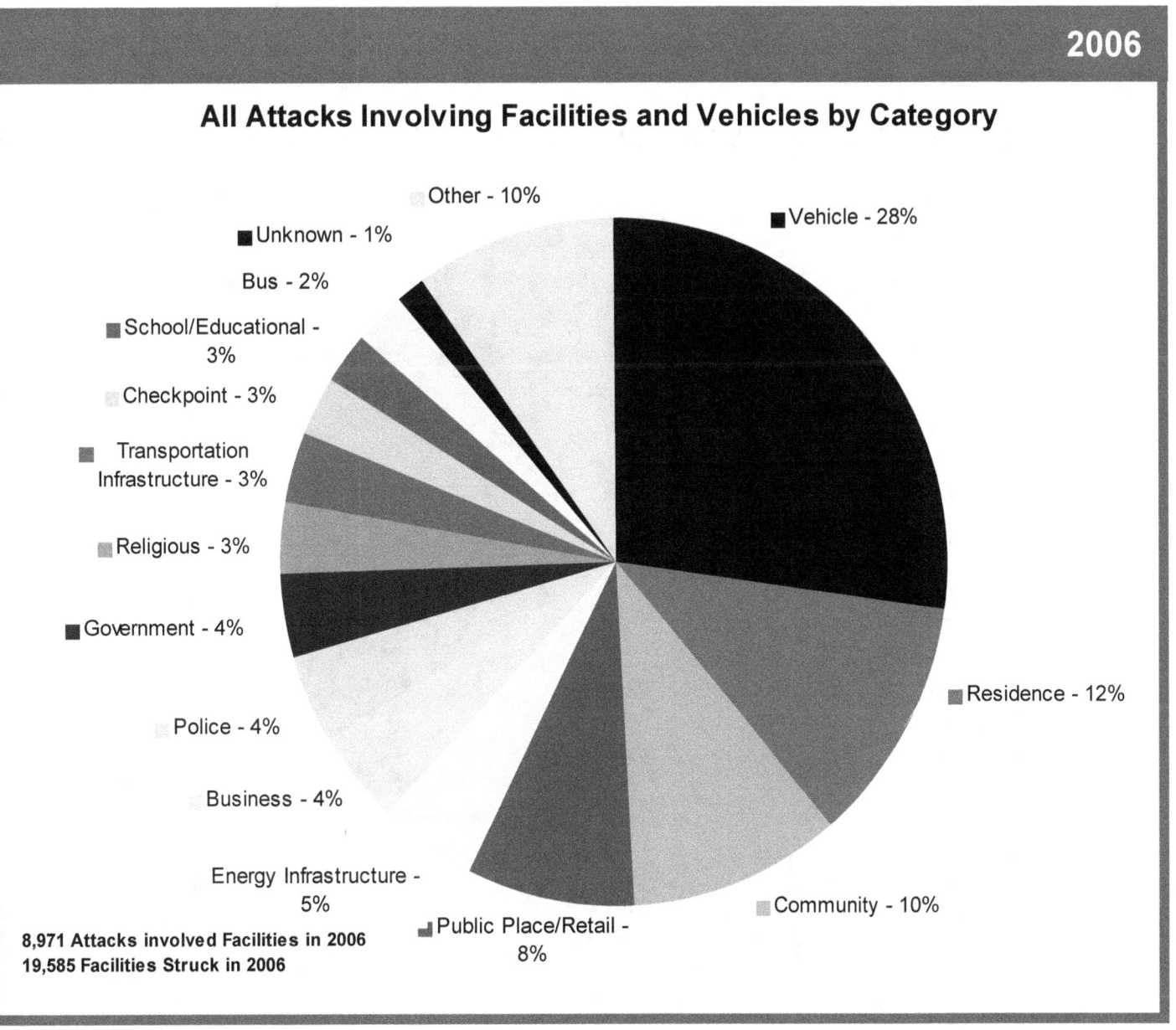

All Attacks Involving Facilities and Vehicles by Category

Other - 10%

Unknown - 1%

Bus - 2%

School/Educational - 3%

Checkpoint - 3%

Transportation Infrastructure - 3%

Religious - 3%

Government - 4%

Police - 4%

Business - 4%

Energy Infrastructure - 5%

Public Place/Retail - 8%

Vehicle - 28%

Residence - 12%

Community - 10%

8,971 Attacks involved Facilities in 2006
19,585 Facilities Struck in 2006

Incidents & Fatalities Comparison between 2005 & 2006

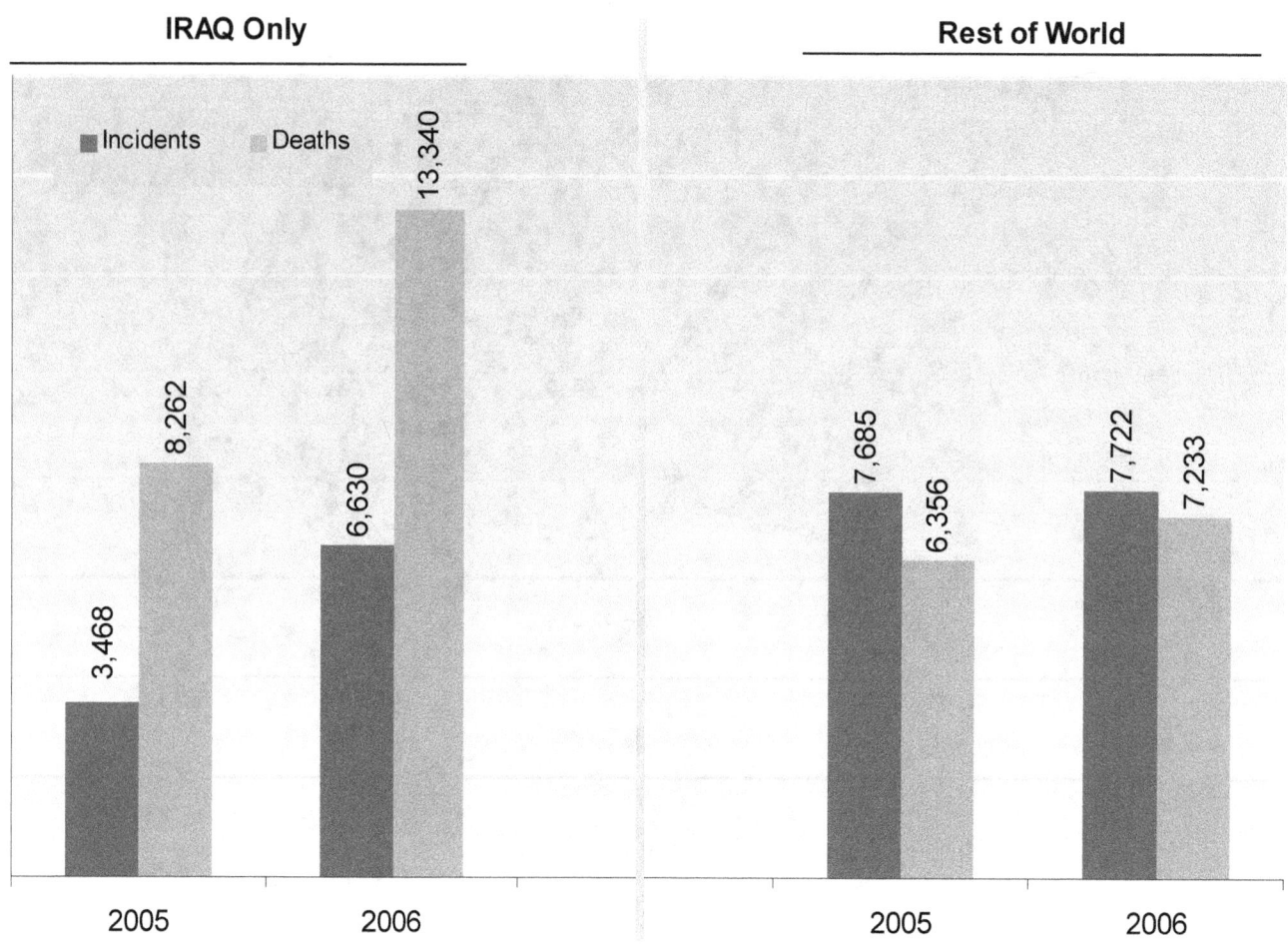

Africa

Within this region, which does not include North Africa, the number of incidents in 2006 was up 64 percent in 2006 from 2005, with incidents rising from 256 to 422.

- Fatalities were up 87 percent, rising from 879 to 1,643.
- Injured victims were up 74 percent, increasing from 666 to 1,162.
- Kidnappings rose substantially, by about 382 percent, from 232 to 1,118.

Terrorism in **Sudan**, **Nigeria**, **Chad**, and the **Democratic Republic of Congo** accounted for most of the increases in both incidents and victims. Terrorism in these countries resulted in 61 percent of all of the incidents in trans-Sahara and sub-Sahara Africa during 2006, and terrorism in these countries accounted for 85 percent of the killed, 49 percent of the wounded, and 94 percent of the kidnapping victims in this region of the world.

- Attacks by the Janjaweed, an Arab militia group, against noncombatants in the *Darfur* region of **Sudan** were reported more often in open sources, rising from four in 2005 to 28 reported incidents in 2006. Fatalities were up as well—716 were reportedly killed in 2006 while only 157 were reported as killed in 2005.
- Oil industry-related kidnappings in **Nigeria** were up, with 25 in 2006, several more than the three reported in 2005. Consequently, the reported number of kidnapped victims in these kidnappings skyrocketed as well, to 203 from 14 in 2005.

Twenty-eight Incidents of 10 or more Deaths

Most of these incidents, 17, occurred in **Sudan** and they were widely believed to be carried out by the Janjaweed militia group, according to open sources. The largest and deadliest attack in this Africa region occurred over a 10 day period in November in eastern **Chad,** during which 400 civilians were killed and 10,000 were displaced apparently by both Chadian and Sudanese Arab militias, according to open sources.

January

15 Nigeria
> In Benisede, Bayelsa, armed assailants detonated explosives at a Shell Petroleum Development Company oil flow station, causing severe damage to the station while killing 14 soldiers and an unknown number of civilian Shell staff members. No group claimed responsibility.

30 Sudan

On or about 30 January 2006, on the road between Kabkabiyah and Al Fashir, in Shamal Darfur, armed assailants killed 22 police reservists and wounded 18 others. No group claimed responsibility, but it was widely believed the Sudan Liberation Movement/Army (SLM/A) was responsible.

March

16 Guinea-Bissau

Near Sao Domingos, a bus drove over a landmine that exploded, killing 11 civilians, injuring 12 others, and damaging the bus. No group claimed responsibility.

April

13 Sudan

In Karamagay, Janub Darfur, assailants killed 15 civilians wounded 11 others, and stole 2177 head of livestock. No group claimed responsibility, although it was widely believed that the Sudanese Janjaweed was responsible.

16 Sudan

In Sha'riyah, Janub Darfur, assailants killed 17 civilians, injured 13 others, and stole approximately 10 head of livestock. No group claimed responsibility.

May

16 Sudan

In Kutum, Shamal Darfur, assailants attacked three villages, killing at least 15 civilians. No group claimed responsibility, although it was widely believed that the Janjaweed militia was responsible.

July

3 Sudan

In Hamrat al-Sheikh, Shamal Kurdufan, armed assailants clashed with the local security force, killing eight police officers, two security officers, and two civilians and destroying several buildings. A newly formed group, National Redemption Front (NRF), claimed responsibility for the attack.

September

18 Somalia

In Baidoa, Bay, a vehicle-borne improvised explosive device (VBIED) exploded at a building housing the interim parliament as the President of the Transitional

Federal Government was leaving the building, killing 12 civilians, including the president's brother. As many as 10 others were wounded, and at least six vehicles were destroyed. Following the attack, police responded and engaged in a gun battle with assailants. No group claimed responsibility.

October

3 Sudan

In Qurayd, Janub Darfur, assailants killed 11 civilians. No group claimed responsibility, although the African Union reported that the Sudan Liberation Movement/Army (SLA/SLM) and the Justice and Equality Movement were responsible.

10 Chad

Between about 10 October 2006 and 20 October 2006, armed assailants attacked 10 villages, killing 40 civilians. As a result, 3,000 civilians were displaced by the violence. No group claimed responsibility, although it was widely believed that the Janjaweed Militia was responsible.

15 Ethiopia

In Beshasha neighborhood of Jima, assailants armed with machetes attacked a Christian congregation, beheading and killing 10 civilians and wounding 30 others. No group claimed responsibility, although it was widely believed unidentified Islamic extremists were responsible.

19 Sudan

On 19 October and 20 October 2006, in Juba, Bahr al Jabal, armed assailants fired upon and killed 42 civilians, wounded 16 others, and damaged three vehicles. No group claimed responsibility, although it was widely believed that the Lord's Resistance Army (LRA) was responsible.

29 Sudan

On 29 October 2006 and 30 October 2006, in Western Darfur, between 300 and 500 armed assailants attacked nine communities, killing 33 children, 28 civilians, and two police officers and causing unspecified damage. No group claimed responsibility, although it was widely believed that the Janjaweed Militia was responsible.

November

4 Chad

From 4 November 2006 to about 13 November 2006, in eastern Chad, assailants attacked 60 villages, killing more than 400 civilians and one aid worker and wounding 100 other civilians. The assailants also destroyed food stores and livestock and burned down villages and residences. The violence displaced approximately 10,000 people. No group claimed responsibility, although it was widely believed that Chadian and Sudanese Arab militias, including Janjaweed Militia, Toboros, and Bachmarga, were responsible.

11 Sudan

In the Sirba region, Gharb Darfur, approximately 300 assailants attacked several villages, killing approximately 32 civilians and wounding between 18 and 40 others. The assailants also burned down 200 residences and stole 500 cows. No group claimed responsibility, although it was widely believed the Janjaweed Militia was responsible.

11 Sudan

Between about 11 and 13 November 2006, in Muhajiriyah, armed assailants attacked several villages, killing 80 civilians and causing unspecified damage. No group claimed responsibility, although it was widely believed the Janjaweed Militia was responsible.

12 Sudan

In South Darfur, armed assailants attacked two villages, killing 15 civilians and causing unspecified damage. No group claimed responsibility, although it was widely believed the Janjaweed Militia was responsible.

12 Sudan

On or about 12 November 2006, in Bir Daqiq, Gharb Darfur, assailants attacked a village, killing 12 civilians and wounding 17 others. The assailants also burned down 29 residences and looted 93 others. No group claimed responsibility, although it was widely believed the Janjaweed Militia was responsible.

20 Sudan

In Umm Bayi, Janub Darfur, armed assailants attacked a village, killing 80 civilians and causing unspecified damage. No group claimed responsibility, although it was widely believed the Janjaweed Militia was responsible.

25 Chad

On 25 November 2006, in the morning, in Abeche, Ouaddai, assailants attacked a community, killing 20 soldiers and 20 civilians and causing unspecified damage. The Union of Forces for Democracy and Development claimed responsibility.

25 Democratic Republic of the Congo

Between about 25 and 29 November 2006, in Sake, Nord Kivu, assailants attacked and took over a community, killing nine soldiers and one civilian, wounding 21 soldiers and 20 civilians, and causing unspecified damage. No group claimed responsibility, although it was widely believed that dissident Army troops were responsible.

28 Sudan

On or about 28 November 2006, in Gharb Kurdufan, armed assailants attacked two communities, killing 32 civilians and causing unspecified damage. No group claimed responsibility, although it was widely believed the Sudan Liberation Movement (SLM) was responsible.

December

4 Sudan

In Shek Gubah, Darfur, assailants fired upon and killed at least 41 civilians. No group claimed responsibility, although it was reported that the Janjaweed were responsible.

9 Sudan

In Sirba, Darfur, assailants fired upon a truck in a refugee convoy, killing 30 civilians and causing unspecified damage. No group claimed responsibility, although the UN said that the Janjaweed were responsible.

15 Sudan

On or about 15 December 2006, in Al Junaynah, Gharb Darfur, assailants killed 15 civilians and wounded five others. No group claimed responsibility, although it was reported that the Janjaweed were responsible.

17 Chad

On or about 17 December 2006, in Aradib, Guera, and Habile, assailants killed at least 15 civilians and eight soldiers. No group claimed responsibility, although it was reported that the Janjaweed were responsible.

23 Sudan

In Tim, assailants killed 18 civilians and kidnapped eight others. No group claimed responsibility.

31 Somalia

On or about 31 December 2006, in Diinsoor Bay, assailants fired upon and killed 10 civilians and kidnapped 10 others. No group claimed responsibility.

East Asia and Pacific

In 2006, incidents in this region, of which about 90 percent occurred in either the **Philippines** or **Thailand**, rose slightly to 1036 from 1007 in 2005. Despite this small rise of incidents, fatalities rose by 12 percent to 854 from 760, and the number of kidnapping victims increased more sharply, by 270 percent, from 62 in 2005 to 229 in 2006.

- There were 906 mostly separatist related incidents in **Thailand** in 2006, down 14 percent from 2005.
- Incidents in the **Philippines** were up 53 percent for 2006, occurring primarily before the death of Abu Sayaf Group (ASG) leader Khadaffy Janjalani in the Fall of 2006.
- There was no high-casualty attack in **Indonesia** in 2006, likely because of more robust regional counterterrorism efforts.

There was only one incident of 10 or more fatalities. On 10 October, a series of three IEDs exploded in Central Mindanao, **Philippines.** One explosion occurred in the market place in Makilala during the celebration marking the 52nd anniversary of the founding of the town, killing 6 civilians and wounding at least 29 others. No group claimed responsibility.

Europe and Eurasia

Although this past summer terrorists in the **United Kingdom** sought but failed to blow-up multiple US-bound commercial planes, no high-casualty attacks causing 10 or more fatalities occurred in Western, Eastern, or Central Europe, and, overall, incidents were down 15 percent in 2006, declining from 780 in 2005 to 659.   Fatalities and injured victims were down 41 and 57 percent, respectively, in 2006, with deaths falling from 373 to 220, and injured victims from 1,898 to 809.

- Incidents fell most notably in **Chechnya** and **Dagestan**, down overall for the year 40 and 59 percent respectively following the successful Russian implementation of an amnesty program beginning in July and effective counterterrorism operations that killed Chechen field commander Basayev on 10 July. In Chechnya, there were 105 attacks in 2005 but only 64 in 2006, while in Dagestan 78 occurred in 2005, and 32 attacks in 2006.
- Attacks by both the IRA in **Northern Ireland** and ETA in **Spain** were down 14 and 10 percent respectively, with IRA attacks dipping to 53, from 62 in 2005.

In other countries attacks rose, doubling in **Kosovo** and up 27 percent overall in **Turkey**. Attacks climbed to 25, from 11 in 2005, in Kosovo, apparently because of ethnic Albanian frustration over independence referendum delays. Attacks in turkey mostly committed by Kongra-Gel (KGK), formerly known as the Kurdistan Workers Party (PKK), increased from 96 in 2005 to 122 in 2006, but fell off dramatically after the 1 October announcement of the unilateral ceasefire initiated by KGK.

Only one incident in this region claimed the life of 10 or more victims.   On the evening of 12 September 2006, in Diyarbakir, **Turkey**, an IED hidden in a thermos exploded at a bus stop near a park, killing two civilians and eight children, while wounding 17 civilians. The Turkish Revenge Brigade (TIT) claimed responsibility for the attack and posted pictures of the bomb preparation on their Web site.

Near East

The majority of terrorism incidents and killed and wounded victims of terror occurred across this region, which stretches from North Africa, through the Arabian Peninsula, the Levant, and Iraq, and terminates in Iran. Attacks across the region were up 83 percent, rising to nearly 7,800, as compared with 4,222 in 2005. Fatalities rose by 57 percent, from about 8700 in 2005 to nearly 13,700 in 2006. The number of injured nearly doubled, from 13,534 in 2005 to over 25,800 last year.

The upswing in terrorism in **Iraq** during 2006 accounts for the largest percentage of these incidents and was the main factor behind increases in incidents of terror, and dead and wounded victims worldwide during the past year. Violence intensified against noncombatants as sectarian violence swept through **Iraq** at high levels following the terrorist attack claimed by AQI against the Golden Dome Mosque, a Shiite holy shrine.

- When compared with 2005, much higher percentages stood out among several factors related to the violence in **Iraq** in 2006—incidents were up 91 percent; fatalities, by 91 percent; wounded victims, by 98 percent; and kidnapped victims, by 320 percent.
- Most incidents—about 56 percent—occurred in the Baghdad and the adjacent Diyala Provinces.
- Although in most cases victims in **Iraq** were reported as individuals, civilians or some other general descriptor, open-sources in 2006 more often included reports that listed educators, police, and government employees as victims, up 430, 66, and 20 percent, respectively, from those reported in 2005.
- Although suicide attacks declined by 33 percent in 2006 to 236 from 354 in 2005, these attacks more than doubled in the second half of 2006 with new AQI leader Abu Ayyub al-Masri, reportedly an explosives expert, in charge of AQI following al-Zarqawi's death in June.
- Mortar, IED, and VBIED attacks in 2006 went up 122, 159, and 37 percent respectively, from those in 2005. In at least 28 percent of the mortar attacks, residential areas were the intended targets. Mortar attacks climbed to 586 from 263, IED attacks swelled to 1659 from 639, and VBIED attacks rose markedly, to 684 from 497 in 2005.
- A new CBRN method of attack was introduced in Iraq during 2006, presaging wave of these attacks in 2007. According to an Iraqi Interior Ministry explosives expert, a large VBIED attack that included chemicals was attempted in Sadr City on 23 November 2006.

Major developments in the **Arab-Israeli** conflict triggered a rise in incidents, up 52 percent to over a thousand in 2006 for this conflict area, primarily in **Israel**, Gaza Strip, and the West Bank. Fatalities were down by 24 percent last year from 314 to 237, but those injured in 2006 rose 36 percent to 1912 from 1410 in 2005, while kidnappings soared 134 percent, from 32 in 2005 to 75 last year. Israeli related incidents climbed as a result of Israel's military operation in Gaza to recover a kidnapped soldier and the Israeli conflict with Hizballah following the kidnapping of two other Israeli soldiers.

- Hizballah fired approximately 4,000 rockets into **Israel,** resulting in 47 dead and 778 wounded Israelis.
- Rocket attacks by Palestinian groups increased by 433 percent in 2006. These groups, which included HAMAS, Fatah, and the Palestine Islamic Jihad (PIJ), launched 560 rocket attacks in 2006, up from 105 in 2005, that killed six noncombatants and wounded 246, far more than the 73 wounded from such attacks in 2005.

Elsewhere across the region, there were few high-lethality attacks killing 10 or more noncombatants but there were major developments. Al-Qa'ida in the Arabian Peninsula conducted the first-ever terrorist attack against a Saudi Arabia oil facility at the major oil processing plant at Abqaiq on 24 February 2006. Security forces, suffering a few casualties, prevented the attackers from damaging processing capabilities. In North Africa, the al-Qa'ida senior leadership approved the merger with the Salafist Group for Preaching and Combat (GSPC), renamed al-Qa'ida in the Lands of the Islamic Maghreb (AQIM), which subsequently launched its first attack against a US target at La Trappe, **Algeria,** on 10 December. The AQIM remotely detonated a bomb that struck a bus and wounded one of the US passengers who worked for a US company, and subsequently the attackers used small arms to fire at the bus, killing or wounding nine non-US civilians.

Two Hundred and Four Incidents of 10 or more Fatalities

There were two of these attacks in **Iran**, **Algeria**, and **Israel** last year, and one in **Egypt**. All other high-fatality attacks in this region were in Iraq. One or more improvised explosive devices (IEDs) were detonated in 132 of the incidents in **Iraq**, and of all the incidents in **Iraq**, 98 attacks were carried out in Baghdad. High-fatality attacks essentially doubled in Iraq starting in May, ranging from 17 to 22 attacks per month through December.

January

4 Iraq

> In Al Miqdadiyah, Diyala, a suicide bomber wearing an improvised explosive device (IED) and armed assailants using mortars attacked the funeral for the

nephew of a Shiite politician, killing 36 civilians and wounding 42 others. No group claimed responsibility.

5 Iraq

At 10:15 AM, in Karbala', a suicide bomber, wearing an IED, attacked a crowd of Shia pilgrims and street vendors outside the Imam Hussein shrine, killing 52 civilians (48 Iraqis, 4 Iranians) and one child, wounding 148 other civilians, and damaging several vendor facilities. AQI claimed responsibility.

5 Iraq

In Ar Ramadi, Al Anbar, a suicide bomber wearing an IED attacked a line of 1,000 civilians waiting at a police recruitment screening center, killing 56 civilians and two US soldiers and wounding 60 civilians and two US soldiers. Although no group claimed responsibility, US authorities suspected AQI was responsible.

9 Iraq

In Nidhal District, central Baghdad, two suicide bombers disguised as Iraqi police officers and wearing IEDs, attacked the National Police Day celebration being observed at the Interior Ministry building, killing 29 police officers and wounding 25 others. The ceremonies were being observed by US Ambassador Khalilzad, Iraqi Interior Minister Bayan Jabr, and Iraqi Defense Minister Sadoun al-Dulaimi, none of whom were injured. AQI claimed responsibility.

17 Iraq

North of Baghdad, assailants kidnapped 43 Sunni rejected police recruits by forcing their bus to stop. The bodies of 13 of the recruits were found the same day with multiple bullet wounds. On 23 January 2006, the bodies of 23 more recruits were found with bullet wounds. On 2 February 2006, the body of one police recruit was found near Ad Dujayl, three bodies were found east of Baghdad, Iraq, and two bodies were found north of Baghdad, Iraq. One hostage survived after being left for dead by the assailants. No group claimed responsibility.

17 Iraq

In At Tarimiyah, Salah ad Din governorate, a joint US/Iraqi military patrol found the bodies of six police officers and five Iraqi soldiers, all of whom had been bound, blindfolded, and executed. No group claimed responsibility.

18 Iraq

Near Ad Dujayl, Salah ad Din, assailants killed 30 civilians who had been stopped at hastily-established illegal roadblocks and dragged from their vehicles. No group claimed responsibility.

19 Iraq

In Saadoun District of central Baghdad, in a coordinated attack a suicide bomber detonated an IED at a crowded coffee shop and seconds later a roadside command-initiated vehicle-borne improvised explosive device (VBIED) was detonated outside a restaurant as a police patrol passed, killing 29 civilians, wounding 20 others, and causing significant damage to the coffee shop and unspecified damage to the restaurant. No group claimed responsibility.

27 Iraq

In the predominately Shiite Hurriya District of northwestern Baghdad, armed assailants wearing police uniforms raided several houses and kidnapped 16 Sunni civilians. On 3 February 2006, in northern Baghdad, 14 victims' bodies were found in the back of a truck with multiple bullet wounds. No group claimed responsibility.

29 Iraq

In Al Iskandariyah, Babil, assailants detonated an IED near a candy shop in a Shiite neighborhood, killing 11 civilians, wounding five others, and causing unspecified damage to the shop. No group claimed responsibility.

February

2 Iraq

In the Al-Amin District of Baghdad, in a double VBIED attack, one VBIED exploded near a gas station and a suicide bomber attacked a market with a VBIED, killing 16 civilians, wounding 90 others, and damaging a gas tanker, several shops and stalls, and the gas station. No group claimed responsibility.

10 Iraq

In the Dora District of southern Baghdad, assailants detonated VBIED outside the Sunni Iskan al-Shaabi mosque, killing 11 civilians, wounding 38 others, and causing unspecified damage. No group claimed responsibility.

14 Iraq

In Balad, assailants attacked a group of Shiite farm workers, killing 10 civilians and one Shiite tribal leader while wounding two civilians. No group claimed responsibility.

20 Iraq

In the Kadhimiya District of Baghdad, a suicide bomber detonated his body-worn IED after he boarded a crowded bus, killing 12 civilians, wounding nine others and damaging the bus. No group claimed responsibility.

21 Iraq

In the Dora District of southern Baghdad, assailants detonated a VBIED in an outdoor market near a police checkpoint, killing 22 civilians, wounding 28 others, and damaging the market, plus at least four vehicles and several buildings. No group claimed responsibility.

22 Iraq

In Al Basrah, assailants dressed in police uniforms kidnapped and killed 12 Sunni civilians (1 Turkish; 2 Tunisian; 1 Saudi; 1 Libyan; 2 Egyptian; 5 Iraqi) being detained at the Maakel Prison on suspicion of being militants. Their bodies were found at three locations in Al Basrah later the same day. No group claimed responsibility.

22 Iraq

In Samarra', Salah ad Din governorate, four assailants, detonated two improvised explosive devices (IEDs) inside the Shiite Askariya (Golden Dome) Mosque, collapsing the dome and damaging the mosque's north wall. As a likely QJBR intended consequence of this attack, on 22 and 23 February 2006, throughout Iraq, assailants attacked at least 184 Sunni mosques with grenades, small arms, mortars, and rocket-propelled grenades (RPGs), killing 12 Sunni imams and seven Sunni civilian worshippers, kidnapping 14 Sunni imams, and causing substantial damage to many of the mosques. On 24 February 2006, near An Nasiriyah, Dhi Qar, Iraq, the body of one of the kidnapped clerics was found. No group claimed responsibility, but it was widely believed that AQI was responsible for the Askariya Mosque attack and Shiite extremists for the country-wide attacks that followed.

23 Iraq

In Ba'qubah, Diyala, assailants detonated a probable command-initiated IED hidden in a soup vendor's handcart near an Iraqi Army patrol in the central market, killing eight Iraqi soldiers and eight civilians, wounding four Iraqi soldiers and 11 civilians, and causing unspecified damage to the public market. The Mujahidin Shura Council in Iraq (MSC) [Majlis Shura Mujahidin fi al-'Iraq] claimed responsibility.

25 Iraq

In Buhriz, Diyala, assailants forcibly entered the home of a Shiite family and fired upon the occupants, killing 13 civilians and causing unspecified damage. No group claimed responsibility.

26 Iraq

In the Dora and Saidiya Districts of Baghdad, assailants attacked two Shiite residential districts with eleven mortar rounds, killing 18 civilians, wounding 51 others, and damaging approximately eight homes. No group claimed responsibility.

28 - Iraq

In the Hurriya District of Baghdad, assailants detonated a roadside VBIED near the Shiite Abdel Hadi Chalabi Mosque and public market, killing 23 civilians, wounding 55 others, and causing unspecified damage to the mosque and market. No group claimed responsibility.

28 - Iraq

In the Al-Amin District of Baghdad, a suicide bomber wearing an IED attacked a crowd lined up at a kerosene distribution point, killing 23 civilians and wounding 51 others. No group claimed responsibility.

March

1 Iraq

In the New Baghdad District, eastern Baghdad, assailants detonated a roadside VBIED near a police checkpoint, killing 26 civilians, wounding 68 others, and causing unspecified damage to the checkpoint. No group claimed responsibility.

2 Iraq

In Ad Dawr, Salah ad Din, armed assailants attacked a police checkpoint, killing seven Iraqi soldiers and four police officers, causing unspecified damage to the checkpoint, and setting fire to several police vehicles. No group claimed responsibility.

2 Iraq

In Nahrawan, Diyala, armed assailants attacked two brick factories, killing 19 Shiite employees and damaging several residences. Although no group claimed responsibility, authorities suspected Sunni extremists perpetrated the attack as part of the spiraling sectarian violence initiated by the Askariya Mosque bombing on 22 February 2006.

10 Iraq

In Al Fallujah, a suicide bomber attacked a joint US and Iraqi police checkpoint with a VBIED, killing five police officers, two civilians, one US soldier, one Iraqi soldier, and one child and causing unspecified damage to several civilian cars and the checkpoint. No group claimed responsibility.

12 Iraq

In Sadr City, Baghdad, assailants launched a coordinated, nearly-simultaneous attack against the Mreidi, Kayara, Dagher, and al-Ula public markets with as many as six VBIEDs, including one suicide VBIED, and four mortar rounds, killing 64 civilians, wounding approximately 290 others, and causing extensive damage to all four markets and several homes and vehicles. Another VBIED was discovered and defused, causing no further injuries or damage. No group claimed responsibility.

16 Iran

Near Zahedan, Sistan va Baluchestan, assailants posing as police officers and soldiers set up a barricade on the Zabol-Zahedan highway. The assailants stopped several cars at the barricade and attacked the drivers and passengers, killing 22 government and provincial officials, wounding the governor of Zahedan, his deputy, and five other officials, kidnapping seven others, and causing unspecified damage to several vehicles. On or about 2 November 2006, the last of the seven kidnapped officials was released. The others had previously been released in three phases. Jundullah (Soldiers of God) claimed responsibility.

21 Iraq

In Al Miqdadiyah, Diyala, a large number of armed assailants attacked a police station, a courthouse, and a municipal council compound with small arms, rocket-propelled grenades (RPGs), and mortars, killing 18 police officers and one courthouse security guard, wounding 13 police officers, setting fire to 18 police vehicles and part of the municipal council building, and causing unspecified damage to the courthouse and police buildings. Two of the police casualties were Interior Ministry commandos who were attempting to reinforce the police station when they were attacked with a roadside improvised explosive device (IED) on the outskirts of town. The Mujahidin Shura Council in Iraq (MSC) claimed responsibility.

23 Iraq

In central Baghdad, Iraq, a suicide bomber detonated a VBIED inside the police major crimes unit headquarters, killing 15 civilians and 10 police officers, wounding 35 police officers and civilians, and causing unspecified damage. No group claimed responsibility.

26 Iraq

Near Tall al-Sakher, Salah ad Din, assailants in three vehicles attacked a group of young men, killing 18 of them. Their bodies were found later along a road. No group claimed responsibility.

27 Iraq

Near Tall Afar, a suicide bomber attacked a group of civilians waiting outside an army recruiting center on the Iraqi Tamarat army base, killing 40 civilians, wounding 30 others, and causing unspecified damage. The Mujahidin Shura Council in Iraq (MSC) claimed responsibility.

April

3 Iraq

In the Sha'ab District of Baghdad, a suicide bomber attacked the Shiite al-Shruqi mosque as worshippers were leaving evening prayers, killing ten civilians, wounding 38 others, and causing unspecified damage to the mosque. No group claimed responsibility, although authorities believed Sunni extremists were responsible.

4 Iraq

In the Shiite Habibiya District of Baghdad, assailants detonated a roadside VBIED near a used car lot surrounded by several food vendors, killing ten civilians, wounding 28 others, damaging several businesses, and destroying 11 vehicles. No group claimed responsibility.

6 Iraq

In Najaf, assailants detonated a roadside probably remote-controlled VBIED 300 meters from the Imam Ali Mosque, near the Wadi Salam cemetery, killing 15 civilians and wounding 42 others, destroying ten vehicles, and causing unspecified damage to the cemetery. No group claimed responsibility.

7 Algeria

In Al-Mani'aa, Ghardaia province, assailants attacked a convoy of vehicles carrying customs agents, killing 13 of the agents, wounding 10 others, and destroying their vehicles. No group claimed responsibility

7 Iraq

In the Kadhimiya District of northern Baghdad, four suicide bombers attacked and damaged the Shiite Buratha Mosque as Friday afternoon prayers were ending, killing 87 civilians, two children, and one journalist while wounding 162 civilians, and two journalists. No group claimed responsibility.

12 Iraq

North of Ba'qubah, Diyala, a suicide bomber using a VBIED attacked the Shia Huweder Mosque from which worshippers were leaving, killing 31 civilians, wounding 70 others, and causing unspecified damage to the mosque and a nearby public market. No group claimed responsibility.

13 Iraq

In the predominantly Shiite Shu'la District of western Baghdad, assailants detonated a roadside probably remote-controlled VBIED near a public vegetable market, killing 15 civilians, wounding 22 others, and causing unspecified damage to the public market. No group claimed responsibility.

13 Iraq

In Al Basrah, assailants kidnapped 11 businessmen working on a reconstruction project and employed by the Al-Fayha Company. Later that same day, in Al Basrah police found their bodies, all of which had sustained bullet wounds. No group claimed responsibility.

16 Iraq

In Al Mahmudiyah, Babil, assailants detonated a roadside VBIED near a Shiite mosque in a public market, killing 11 civilians, wounding 23 others, and causing unspecified damage to the market and mosque. No group claimed responsibility although authorities believed Sunni extremists were responsible.

17 Israel

In Tel Aviv, a suicide bomber detonated an IED outside of a restaurant, killing 10 civilians and one American teenager, wounding at least 66 civilians, and damaging the restaurant. An unknown number of other children were among the victims. Al-Quds Brigades of Palestinian Islamic Jihad (PIJ) claimed responsibility in an Internet posting.

23 Algeria

Near El Kassa, assailants detonated an IED in front of a van, severely damaging it. The assailants then fired upon the passengers, killing nine municipal guards and one civilian and wounding eight other guards. No group claimed responsibility, although it was widely believed that the Salafist Group for Call and Combat (GSPC) was responsible.

23 Iraq

In Ar Ramadi, assailants kidnapped 15 police recruits who were to work in Ar Ramadi, Al Anbar, Iraq, for a special Interior Ministry unit. On 24 April 2006, in Abu Ghurayb, Al Anbar governorate, police found their dead bodies inside a small truck. They had been tortured and sustained multiple bullet wounds. No group claimed responsibility, but authorities believed Sunni extremists were responsible.

24 Egypt

In Dahab, in a simultaneous and coordinated attack, three Egyptian suicide bombers detonated IEDs at three locations in the resort city. The first suicide bomber detonated his IED outside the beachfront Al-Capone restaurant, the second detonated his IED outside the Ghazala supermarket, and third detonated his IED next to a popular pedestrian footbridge. The three bombings occurred within less than one minute, killing at least 17 civilians (14 Egyptians; 1 Swiss; 1 Lebanese; 1 Russian) and one German child, wounding at least 62 civilians (42 Egyptians; 5 Danes, 3 British; 2 Italians; 2 Germans; 2 French; 1 South Korean; 1 Lebanese; 1 Palestinian; 1 American; 1 Israeli; 1 Australian), and severely damaging at least 10 shops and several hotels, restaurants, and supermarkets. No group claimed responsibility, although it was widely believed Al-Tawhid Wal-Jihad (Unity and Jihad Group in Egypt) was responsible.

May

2 Iraq

In Ar Ramadi, a suicide bomber attacked the convoy of the governor of Al Anbar, Maamoun Rashid Sami al-Alwani, in an assassination employing a VBIED, killing probably 10 civilians, wounding the governor and five security guards and damaging seven vehicles. When a US convoy responded, it came under small arms fire that wounded one Marine. No group claimed responsibility.

3 Iraq

In Al Fallujah, a suicide bomber detonated an IED in a police recruiting compound, killing between 13 and 16 civilians and two police officers and wounding approximately 30 civilians. No group claimed responsibility.

4 Iraq

In Sadr City, Baghdad, an IED exploded outside of the courthouse, killing up to 10 civilians and one child, wounding between 39 and 50 civilians, and two police officers, while damaging several nearby businesses. No group claimed responsibility.

5 Iraq

In Baghdad, assailants detonated a VBIED near a gas station, killing 11 civilians, wounding 22 others, and causing unspecified damage to the station. No group claimed responsibility.

In Karbala', a suicide bomber used a VBIED to attack a government building, killing 15-21 people, wounding 19-55 others, and damaging at least 12 vehicles. No group claimed responsibility.

7 Iraq

In the Adhamiya District of northern Baghdad, a suicide bomber detonated a VBIED against a military patrol, killing 10 soldiers and wounding up to 30 people. No group claimed responsibility.

9 Iraq

In the Al Wihdad neighborhood of Tal Afar, a suicide bomber detonated a VBIED in a public market, killing between 15 and 52 people and wounding between 35 and 134 others. Victims included children, civilians, police officers and Iraqi troops. The blast left a large hole in the market area. No group claimed responsibility.

10 Iraq

Near Ba'qubah, Diyala, assailants stopped a minibus carrying employees of the state-run Diyala Electronics Company, then killed all of the men. When rescuers from another company bus opened the minibus door, an IED exploded. In total, between 11 and 12 civilians were killed, and between three and six others and between one and four police officers were wounded. No group claimed responsibility.

13 Iran

In Kerman, as many as 30 assailants set up a barricade on the Kerman-Bam Road and stopped four civilian vehicles. The assailants forced all the occupants out of the vehicles then fired upon the civilians, killing all 11, and set the four vehicles on fire. The assailants then fired upon a passing vehicle, killing one civilian, wounding a child, and damaging the vehicle. Jundullah (Soldiers of God) claimed responsibility.

14 Iraq

In western Baghdad, suicide bombers attacked the motorcade of the Electricity Minister with two VBIEDs as it neared a checkpoint outside the Baghdad International Airport, killing 14 civilians, wounding six others, and damaging several civilian vehicles. No group claimed responsibility.

16 Iraq

In the predominantly Shiite Sha'ab District, northern Baghdad, assailants, firing from a minibus, killed five Mahdi Army Shiite Militia members in a parking lot near a public market. As civilians rushed to the parking lot to respond to the shooting, the assailants detonated a probably remote-controlled VBIED next to an oil tanker, causing the tanker to explode, killing 19 civilians, wounding 36 others, and damaging several civilian vehicles parked nearby. No group claimed responsibility although authorities suspect sectarian violence.

20 Iraq

In Sadr City, Baghdad, assailants detonated a probably remote-controlled IED hidden inside a garbage bag near a food stand where day laborers had gathered for breakfast. The explosion killed 19 civilians, wounded 58 others, and damaged one business. Although no group claimed responsibility, authorities suspected Sunni extremists were responsible.

21 Iraq

In the Karrada District of central Baghdad, a suicide bomber wearing an IED attacked the Safwan Restaurant, killing nine civilians and 3 police officers, wounding 17 civilians, and severely damaging the restaurant. The Mujahidin Shura Council in Iraq (MSC) [Majlis Shura Mujahidin fi al-'Iraq] claimed responsibility.

22 Iraq

In Karrada District of central Baghdad, assailants detonated a roadside improvised explosive device (IED) near a passing US military patrol, killing ten civilians but causing no damage. No group claimed responsibility.

23 Iraq

In the Tunis District of northern Baghdad, assailants detonated a roadside probably remote-controlled VBIED outside the Shiite Imam al-Muntadher Mosque as worshippers were leaving night prayers, killing 11 civilians, and wounding nine others, and damaging a nearby sandwich shop. Although no group claimed responsibility, authorities believed Sunni extremists conducted the attack as part of the ongoing sectarian violence.

29 Iraq

In the predominately Sunni Adhamiya District of northern Baghdad, assailants detonated a roadside, probably remote-controlled VBIED near the Sunni Abu Hanifa Mosque, killing 11 civilians and one child, wounding 24 other civilians, and causing minor damage to the mosque. No group claimed responsibility but authorities believe this attack was perpetrated by Shiite extremists.

29 Iraq

Near Al Khalis, Diyala, assailants detonated a roadside IED near a bus transporting workers to an Iraqi military base, killing 14 civilians, wounding 17 others, and damaging the bus. No group claimed responsibility.

29 Iraq

In the predominantly Sunni, Adhamiya District of northern Baghdad, assailants detonated a roadside VBIED near the Ibin al-Haitham College as an Iraqi Army patrol passed, killing 12 university students and wounding 20 civilians and 4 Iraqi soldiers. No group claimed responsibility.

30 Iraq

In predominately Shiite Husayniyah, Baghdad, assailants detonated a roadside, probably remote-controlled VBIED near a public market, killing 25 civilians, wounding 65 others, and causing unspecified damage to the market place. Police defused a second VBIED probably positioned to target first responders, causing no further injuries or damage. Although no group claimed responsibility authorities suspect Sunni extremists perpetrated the attack.

30 Iraq

In the Al-Nadir district of Al Hillah, Babil, a suicide bomber attacked a car showroom with a VBIED, killing 12 civilians, wounding 36 others, and causing extensive damage to the car dealership. No group claimed responsibility, but authorities suspect this attack may have had sectarian motivations.

June

1 Iraq

In the Dora District of southern Baghdad, assailants attacked the area with 12 mortar rounds in two successive attacks, killing one child and between eight and 12 civilians, wounding between 43 and 69 other civilians and damaging a restaurant, a vegetable market, and four residences. No group claimed responsibility.

3 Iraq

In Al Basrah, a suicide bomber detonated a VBIED near the Hamza market, killing 33 civilians, wounding between 62 and 80 others, and damaging the market and several businesses and vehicles. No group claimed responsibility.

4 Iraq

In Ayn Laylin, Diyala, assailants stopped two minibuses and a truck at an illegal checkpoint, removed the passengers and fired upon and killed 12 Shiite students and between nine and 14 Shiite civilians and wounded one other civilian. No group claimed responsibility.

4 Iraq

On or about 4 June 2006, in the Al Unayadah district of Ba'qubah, Diyala, assailants fired upon a group of civilians, killing 19 civilians and wounding two others. No group claimed responsibility.

4 Iraq

On or about 4 June 2006, in the Abu Dishir District of southwestern Baghdad, assailants in several attacks killed 18 Shiite civilians. No group claimed responsibility, although it is widely believed that Sunni extremists were responsible.

5 Iraq

> In central Al Basrah, assailants, in a series of random attacks, fired upon and killed 14 civilians and wounded eight others in several areas of the city, including near Basra General Hospital. No group claimed responsibility.

5 Iraq

> In Qara Tapa, Diyala, assailants stopped a bus at an illegal checkpoint, removed the 26 passengers, separated them into groups according to their religious sects, and killed 22 Shiite Turkmen. No group claimed responsibility.

6 Iraq

> Between 3 and 6 June 2006, in Baghdad, assailants attacked and killed 11 Health Ministry employees and wounded 20 others. No group claimed responsibility.

8 Iraq

> In the New Baghdad District, a roadside IED exploded at a large outdoor produce market, killing 13 civilians, wounding between 28 and 39 others, and causing unspecified damage to the market and severe damage to several shops. No group claimed responsibility.

8 Iraq

> In the Sha'ab area in the predominately Sunni Adhamiya District of northern Baghdad, a VBIED exploded at the Shalal market, killing 10 Sunni civilians, wounding between 10 and 42 others, and causing unspecified damage to the market and several properties in the area. No group claimed responsibility.

12 Iraq

> In Baghdad, assailants kidnapped 14 employees from an electricity plant. On 22 June 2006, authorities found their bodies in the city morgue. The Mujahideen Shura Council in Iraq (MSC) claimed responsibility.

13 Iraq

> In Kirkuk, in a coordinated operation, assailants used VBIEDs and IEDs to attack several targets, mostly police, killing seven police officers, 25 civilians, one translator for the British Embassy and five other people, and wounding nine police officers, 43 civilians, four guards and 23 other people. The incident damaged several residences, an open-air market, six vehicles and two offices of the Patriotic Union of Kurdistan (PUK). The Mujahidin Shura Council (MSC) claimed responsibility.

15 Iraq

At about 3:00 PM, in the Yarmuk district of western Ba'qubah, Diyala, assailants stopped a bus, forced everybody off and then killed the driver and nine other civilians, all Shiites. No group claimed responsibility.

15 Iraq

In Ba'qubah, Diyala, assailants fired upon and killed 10 civilians who were standing across from the al-Rahmah Hospital. No group claimed responsibility.

16 Iraq

In the Utayfiya District of northern Baghdad, a suicide bomber attacked the Shiite Buratha Mosque with an IED, killing 13 civilians, wounding 28 others, and damaging the mosque interior. Although no group claimed responsibility, authorities suspect AQI perpetrated the attack.

17 Iraq

In the Dora District of southern Baghdad, assailants detonated a roadside probably remote-controlled VBIED near a police checkpoint, killing 12 civilians, and wounding 38 others, and causing unspecified damage to the checkpoint. The Mujahidin Shura Council in Iraq (MSC) [Majlis Shura Mujahidin fi al-'Iraq] claimed responsibility.

21 Iraq

In At Taji, assailants kidnapped approximately 64 Ministry of Industry factory workers employed at the al-Nasr General Complex as they were leaving work, by hijacking five buses and several cars transporting them home. Subsequently, 30 hostages, mostly Sunni women, were released. On 22 June 2006, Iraqi police raided a farm near Baghdad, Iraq, and freed 17 other hostages. On 28 June 2006, authorities stated a total of 11 of the employees had been found bound, tortured and with bullet wounds. In an ambiguous internet statement, the Mujahidin Shura Council in Iraq (MSC) [Majlis Shura Mujahidin fi al-'Iraq] claimed responsibility, but it was not clear if they were referring to this incident.

23 Iraq

In the city center of Al Basrah, a suicide bomber attacked a line of vehicles waiting for fuel at a gasoline station on Bashar Street, killing ten civilians, wounding 16 others and two police officers, and damaging several cars, the gas station, and a nearby market. No group claimed responsibility.

23 Iraq

Near Ba'qubah, assailants detonated an IED placed inside a garbage can at the rear entrance to the Sunni Hibhib al-Kabir Mosque, killing 12 civilians, wounding

20 others, and damaging the mosque and several nearby cars. No group claimed responsibility.

26   Iraq

In Kharnabat, Diyala, assailants detonated a roadside, probably remote-controlled VBIED near the town's main square and market, killing 12 civilians and 10 children, wounding 33 other civilians, and damaging the public market. No group claimed responsibility.

26 Iraq

In Al Hillah, Babil, assailants detonated an IED near a public market, killing 15 civilians, wounding 53 other civilians and three children, and damaging the market. No group claimed responsibility.

July

1 Iraq

In Sadr City, Baghdad, assailants detonated a VBIED at the al-Ula or Suq al-Auola market, targeting a mobile police patrol that had already passed by, killing as many as 70 civilians and at least one child, wounding between 87 and 124 civilians and at least one child, and damaging the market, including as many as 40 stores, the fronts of several buildings, and dozens of vehicles. The group Supporters of the Sunni People (SSP) claimed responsibility.

6 Iraq

In Al Kufah, a suicide bomber attacked Shiite pilgrims by driving his minivan, VBIED, between two buses near the Shia Maytham al-Tammar shrine, killing eight Iranian Shiite pilgrims and four or five Iraqi pilgrims while wounding 22 Iranian pilgrims, between 14 and 25 Iraqi pilgrims, one 16-year-old vender and several other vendors who also were minors. The attack damaged two buses, a vendor's stall, the facade of the shrine, and a nearby cemetery. No group claimed responsibility.

8 Iraq

In the Al-Jihad District of western Baghdad, assailants detonated a VBIED in a public garage near the Shiite Fatima Zahra mosque, killing nine civilians and three children, wounding 18 others, and damaging the mosque, the garage and five parked cars. No group claimed responsibility.

9 Iraq

In the Kasra area of Adhamiya District, northern Baghdad, assailants detonated two VBIEDs in a marketplace near the Shiite Ahl al-Bait (Ahal al-Bait) mosque, killing five police officers and between 14 and 20 civilians, wounding 59 others, and damaging the mosque, the market place, and five vehicles. No group claimed responsibility.

9 Iraq

In the Al-Jihad District of southern Baghdad, roving bands of assailants invaded Sunni homes and set up at least two illegal police checkpoints, forcing Sunnis out of their cars. The attackers fired upon and then hanged three Interior Ministry police commandos, killed between eight and 54 civilians, including several children, and wounded 10 civilians. Some of the victims were tortured with drills, bolts, or nails before they were killed. Several houses were also set on fire. No group claimed responsibility, however it was widely believed that members of Shiite paramilitary groups were responsible.

9 Iraq

In Sadr City, Baghdad, assailants attacked several neighborhoods, killing 11 civilians and wounding 32 others. No group claimed responsibility, however it was widely believed that the Mahdi Army was responsible.

10 Iraq

In Sadr City, Baghdad, assailants detonated a VBIED near both a vehicle repair shop and the Talibiya Communications Center, wounding at least six civilians and damaging the repair shop, an unspecified number of vehicles, and probably the communications center. A suicide bomber then drove into the crowd that had gathered at the first bombing and detonated another VBIED, killing 12 civilians and wounding between 45 and 62 others. Assailants also launched one or two mortar rounds against the community. No group claimed responsibility.

11 Iraq

Near the International (Green) Zone in Baghdad, assailants detonated a roadside remote-controlled VBIED near the Sirwan Restaurant which was quickly followed by two suicide bombers attacking the Simsim restaurant with IEDs, killing 15 civilians and 1 police officer, wounding 13 other civilians, and destroying both restaurants. A convoy carrying a Shiite member of parliament from Muqtada al-Sadr's Party was also passing by at the time of the attacks and may have been targeted as well. The Islamic Army in Iraq (IAI) claimed responsibility for the VBIED attack, adding that one of the suicide bombers detonated the VBIED and the Mujahideen Shura Council in Iraq (MSC) [Majlis Shura Mujahideen fi al-'Iraq] claimed responsibility for both suicide bombers.

11 Iraq

In the Dora District of southern Baghdad, assailants, traveling in two vehicles, attacked a minibus transporting a coffin and Shiite mourners to An Najaf, for a funeral, killing ten civilians, wounding one other, and damaging the minibus. No group claimed responsibility, but it is believed Sunni extremists were responsible.

12 Iraq

In Al Miqdadiyah, Diyala, assailants kidnapped 26 Shiite civilians, described as minibus drivers and quarry workers, at a bus station. Later the same day near the village of Zeham, Iraqi Army troops found the bodies of 24 of the hostages, most of whom had been blindfolded, bound, and fired upon. No group claimed responsibility, but it is believed Sunni extremists were responsible.

14 Iraq

In the Qahira District of northern Baghdad, assailants detonated two IEDs outside the front door of the Sunni Ismail al-Qubaisy Mosque as worshippers were leaving afternoon prayers, killing 14 Sunni civilians, wounding five others, and causing minor damage to the mosque and several parked cars. Shortly after the IED explosion, several mortar rounds were also fired at the mosque. No group claimed responsibility, but it is widely believed that Shiite extremists were responsible.

16 Iraq

In Tozkhurmato, Salah ad Din, a suicide bomber detonated an IED at the Alam Dar coffee shop, killing 28 Shiite civilians, wounding 19 others, and destroying the shop. The Mujahidin Shura Council in Iraq (MSC) [Majlis Shura Mujahidin fi al-'Iraq] claimed responsibility.

17 Iraq

In the Jazaer district of Al Mahmudiyah, assailants attacked the funeral for a Shiite Mahdi Army member, killing nine civilian mourners. The same assailants subsequently attacked a nearby public market with mortars, hand grenades, rocket-propelled grenades (RPGs), and small arms fire, killing 48-72 civilians and three Iraqi soldiers at a checkpoint, wounding 45-90 other civilians, and damaging dozens of market stalls, eight vehicles, at least two homes, and one military checkpoint. The Supporters of the Sunni People (SSP) [Ahel al-Sunnah al-Munasera] claimed responsibility.

18 Iraq

In Al Kufah, a suicide bomber, promising jobs to Shiite day laborers at a gathering place, detonated a VBIED when they moved toward his minivan, killing 59 civilians and wounding 132 others. Six vehicles and two retail shops were also damaged by the explosion. The Mujahidin Shura Council in Iraq (MSC) [Majlis Shura Mujahidin fi al-'Iraq] claimed responsibility.

20 Iraq

In Bayji, Salah ad Din, assailants detonated a probably remote-controlled VBIED parked at a gasoline station. A crowd had gathered around the vehicle after a body was noticed inside, so the explosion killed nine civilians and three police officers, wounded seven other civilians, and damaged the gasoline station. No group claimed responsibility.

23 Iraq

In the predominately Shiite Jamila District of eastern Baghdad, a suicide bomber attacked a gathering site for day laborers. The bomber detonated a VBIED, killing 35 civilians of which some were children, wounding 73 others, and damaging one public market, seven vehicles, ten shops, and one police station. No group claimed responsibility, although Sunni extremists are suspected of perpetrating this attack.

23 Iraq

In central Kirkuk, assailants detonated a roadside, probably remote-controlled VBIED near a courthouse and public market, killing 22 civilians, wounding seven police officers and 157 unspecified people some of whom were judges and lawyers, and damaged the government building, numerous market shops, and at least ten vehicles. No group claimed responsibility.

27 Iraq

In the Karrada District of central Baghdad, assailants, in a coordinated attack, detonated a roadside VBIED in a predominately Shiite neighborhood and subsequently fired at least two mortar rounds and two rockets into the same area. The attack killed 31 civilians, wounded 153 others, and damaged several buildings, including a gas station, an apartment complex, several businesses, a bank, and at least two trucks. Witnesses claimed the mortar rounds came from a predominately Sunni neighborhood in Dora District, Baghdad, Iraq. The al-Sahaba Soldiers (Jamaat Jund al-Shaba), part of the Mujahidin Shura Council in Iraq (MSC) [Majlis Shura Mujahidin fi al-'Iraq], claimed responsibility.

30 Iraq

In the Rasheed District of southern Baghdad, 15 assailants commandeered three minibuses transporting Shiite pilgrims to An Najaf, forced the occupants into a nearby palm grove, and killed 23 civilians. No group claimed responsibility, although Sunni extremists were suspected of perpetrating this attack.

August

1 Iraq

In the Karrada District of central Baghdad, a VBIED exploded near a bank where Iraqi security forces were drawing their monthly salaries. Eight civilians, three police officers, and three soldiers were killed in the explosion. In addition, 37 people were wounded and eight civilian cars were burned as a result of the explosion. No group claimed responsibility.

2 Iraq

In the Al-Amil District of western Baghdad, two improvised explosive devices (IEDs) exploded simultaneously in a soccer stadium while a game was underway, killing 12 children and four civilians and injuring eight children and two civilians. The stadium where the IEDs were planted is opposite a police station, which may have been the target. No group claimed responsibility.

2 Iraq

Along the Baghdad-Wasit highway near Al Kut, assailants attacked a police checkpoint, killing eight civilians and six police officers. No group claimed responsibility.

3 Iraq

In the Al-Amin neighborhood of eastern Baghdad, an IED hidden in a pile of garbage exploded, killing 10 civilians and wounding between 23 and 32 others. No group claimed responsibility.

3 Iraq

In the Shorja District of central Baghdad, a VBIED exploded, killing 12 civilians, wounding 32 others, and damaging the commercial district. No group claimed responsibility.

3 Iraq

In Al Hadr, Ninawa, an assailant detonated a VBIED near a police checkpoint protecting a soccer match, killing seven civilians and three police officers, wounding three civilians and nine police officers, and damaging the checkpoint. No group claimed responsibility.

6 Iraq

In Tikrit, a suicide bomber, wearing an IED, walked into a public hall, and detonated his explosives, killing 15 civilians, wounding 30 others, and causing light damage to the public hall. No group claimed responsibility.

6 Israel

Throughout HaZafon, Katyusha rockets fired from southern Lebanon landed in the region, killing 12 Israeli Defense Force (IDF) reservists, wounding 10 others, and damaging at least 10 communities. Hizballah (Party of God) claimed responsibility.

7 Iraq

In Samarra', a suicide bomber detonated a VBIED near the regional headquarters of an Iraqi police organization, killing 10 police officers, wounding 30 civilians, severely damaging the headquarters building, and destroying three houses and six vehicles. No group claimed responsibility.

8 Iraq

In the Shorja District of central Baghdad, two IEDs exploded nearly simultaneously, killing 10 civilians, wounding 69 others, and causing light damage to three businesses. No group claimed responsibility.

10 Iraq

In An Najaf, a suicide bomber wearing an IED attempted to attack the Shiite Imam Ali Mosque when he detonated his explosives at a police checkpoint in front of the mosque and within a public market, killing 30 Shiite civilians and five police officers, wounding 122 other civilians, and damaging the checkpoint and public market but causing no damage to the mosque. The Soldier's of the Prophet's Companions claimed responsibility.

13 Iraq

At the Al-Qubyasi market in southeastern Baghdad, assailants fired several mortar rounds and detonated three VBIEDs. The first was a suicide motorcycle attack, the second detonated as police arrived, killing 72 civilians, wounding 140 other civilians, of which several were children, and three police officers, and destroying two residences and two businesses. The al-Sahaba Soldiers (Jamaat Jund al-Sahaba) claimed responsibility.

16 Iraq

At about 6:20 PM, on Tunis Street in central Baghdad, two vehicle-borne improvised explosive device (VBIEDs) exploded simultaneously, killing 13 civilians, wounding 55 others, and causing unspecified damage to facilities located nearby. No group claimed responsibility.

20 Iraq

In the Fadhil, Haifa, and Suleikh Districts of central Baghdad, in several separate attacks, armed assailants fired into crowds of Shiite pilgrims and into several residences. Armed assailants also attacked two Shiite mosques and fired mortar rounds that landed on several houses. Approximately 20 civilians and one child were killed, 304 civilians and 10 Iraqi soldiers were wounded, and the mosques and an unspecified number of residences were damaged. No group claimed responsibility.

20 Iraq

In Al Miqdadiyah, Diyala, assailants detonated an IED near a US patrol, killing 11 civilians and setting fire to and damaging a military vehicle. No group claimed responsibility.

27 Iraq

In Al Khalis, Diyala, in a drive-by shooting, assailants in three vehicles attacked a public market and a cafe with small arms fire and rocket-propelled grenades (RPGs), killing 23 Shiite civilians, wounding 18 others, and causing unspecified damage to the market and restaurant. No group claimed responsibility.

28 Iraq

In the Nidhal District of eastern Baghdad, a suicide bomber attacked a police checkpoint outside the Interior Ministry building, killing 13 police officers and 3 civilians, wounding 18 police officers and 29 civilians, and damaging the checkpoint, the Interior Ministry building, and five vehicles. The Mujahideenn Shura Council in Iraq (MSC) [Majlis Shura Mujahideen fi al-'Iraq] claimed responsibility

30 Iraq

In Al Hillah, assailants detonated a VBIED near an Iraqi Army recruitment center, killing between 12 and 17 civilians, wounding between 28 and 39 others, and causing minor damage to the recruitment center. No group claimed responsibility.

30 Iraq

In the predominantly Sunni Shorja District of central Baghdad, assailants detonated a VBIED in the Shorja Market, killing 27 civilians, wounding between 38 and 45 civilians, and damaging several shops and stalls, two vehicles and a restaurant. No group claimed responsibility.

31 Iraq

In the Al-Amin, Baladiyyat, and Qahira Districts, and Sadr City in eastern Baghdad, in a coordinated attack, assailants struck a public market, apartment building, a telephone exchange, a medical center and four other shopping areas with two VBIEDs, four mortar rounds, two rockets, and two IEDs, killing 68 civilians, wounding at least 300 others, and causing extensive property damage. Most of the victims were Shiite. The Soldiers of the Prophet's Companions [Jamaat Jund al-Sahaba] claimed responsibility.

31 Iraq

In Ar Rutbah, Al Anbar, assailants attacked a group of Shiite pilgrims, kidnapping and then killing 14 pilgrims (3 Indians; between 8 and 11 Pakistanis) and their Iraqi Shiite driver. The victims were also tortured. No group claimed responsibility.

September

4 Iraq

In the Bayaa' District of southwestern Baghdad, assailants attacked the industrial quarter, killing 12 civilians and wounding nine others but causing no damage. No group claimed responsibility, although authorities believed that the Mahdi Army was responsible.

7 Iraq

In the Karrada District of central Baghdad, a suicide bomber drove a VBIED into a police fuel depot near Ilwiya Hospital and detonated it, killing 12 police officers, wounding 26 others and 13 civilians, and damaging six police vehicles, 18 civilian vehicles, several shops, and the fuel depot. No group claimed responsibility.

11 Iraq

In the Muthana District of western Baghdad, a suicide bomber, wearing an IED, boarded a minibus full of Iraqi Army recruits outside the Al-Muthana recruiting center and detonated his explosives, killing 16 recruits, wounding seven others, and destroying the minibus. No group claimed responsibility.

13 Iraq

In the Zayoona District of eastern Baghdad, assailants detonated a roadside, probably remote-controlled VBIED near a police station at a passing police patrol responsible for electrical infrastructure security. The attack killed nine civilians and three police officers, wounded 27 civilians and seven police officers, and damaging the police station and several vehicles. The Mujahidin Shura Council in Iraq (MSC) [Majlis Shura Mujahidin fi al-'Iraq] claimed responsibility.

13 Iraq

In the Nidhal District of eastern Baghdad, assailants detonated a roadside, probably remote-controlled VBIED in a parking lot in front of the General Traffic Directorate, killing 14 civilians and five police officers, wounding 62 other civilians, and damaging dozens of vehicles. No group claimed responsibility.

17 Iraq

In Kirkuk, a suicide bomber fired upon civilians and then detonated a VBIED near the police investigation center, killing 17 civilians and two children, wounding 62 other civilians and several police officers and damaging the police center. This is one of five car bombings to occur in Kirkuk on this day. No group claimed responsibility.

17 Iraq

In Al Fallujah, in coordinated attacks, a roadside IED exploded near a police patrol. Later, two VBIEDs exploded near two other police patrols. Shortly after these attacks a mortar round landed in the area of a joint US and Iraqi police base. The attacks in all killed five police officers, five Iraqi soldiers and eight civilians, wounded three other police officers and 12 civilians, and caused some damage to the base. No group claimed responsibility.

18 Iraq

At the Al Hurriyah police station in Ar Ramadi, two suicide bombers detonated VBIEDs where many civilians had gathered to sign up for the police force, killing two police officers and between two and 11 civilians, wounding 18 police officers and eight civilians, and causing damage to the police center. No group claimed responsibility.

18 Iraq

In Tall 'Afar, a suicide bomber detonated the explosive belt he was wearing in a market near civilians waiting for butane gas ration cards, killing two police officers and 19 civilians, wounding 17 civilians, and damaging the market. The Mujahidin Shura Council in Iraq (MSC) claimed responsibility.

19 Iraq

In Sharqat, a VBIED exploded near a passing Iraqi military and police patrol. As civilians gathered around the damaged vehicle, a suicide bomber detonated the IED he was wearing, killing 21 civilians and wounding 50 others. The Mujahidin Shura Council in Iraq (MSC) claimed responsibility.

19 Iraq

In the Abu Dishr neighborhood of southern Baghdad, assailants fired five rockets into a community, killing 10 civilians, wounding 19 others, and damaging five homes. No group claimed responsibility.

20 Iraq

In Samarra', a suicide bomber drove into the home of a tribal leader and detonated a VBIED, killing nine civilians and one child, wounding 26 other civilians and 12 children, and damaging three homes. No group claimed responsibility.

20 Iraq

In the Abu Dishir neighborhood of Baghdad, assailants fired multiple mortar rounds into a community, killing 10 civilians, wounding 20 others, and causing light damage to the community. No group claimed responsibility.

23 Iraq

At 10:00 AM, in Sadr City District, Baghdad, assailants detonated improvised explosive devices (IEDs) next to a kerosene tanker truck, killing 37 civilians and wounding 43 others who were buying supplies for Ramadan. Soldiers of the Prophet's Companions claimed responsibility.

23 Iraq

In Bayji, Salah ad Din, assailants stopped two cars at a checkpoint, taking eight civilians and two police officers hostage. The assailants killed the victims later in the day. No group claimed responsibility.

23 Iraq

Assailants attacked and killed 10 civilian Shia Muslims (4 Indians; 3 Pakistanis; 3 of unknown nationality) as they traveled through Iraq to Syria. The Sunni Islamic extremist group Ansar al-Sunnah claimed responsibility.

27 Iraq

In the predominantly Shiite Hurriya District of northwestern Baghdad, in a drive-by shooting, armed assailants killed 11 civilians and wounded 10 others near a Sunni mosque. No group claimed responsibility.

October

4 Iraq

Near the al-Masuodi School in Camp Sarah District, central Baghdad, assailants detonated two IEDs in front of a convoy of cars belonging to the Industry Minister, killing three bodyguards and damaging several vehicles. When a crowd gathered to tend to casualties from the first attack, a VBIED exploded at a nearby automotive parts market, killing between nine and 18 civilians, wounding 15 police commandos, 11 bodyguards, and between 51 and 63 civilians, and damaging several vehicles, the market, several dozen shops, and several buildings, one of which collapsed. The minister was not in the convoy. No group claimed responsibility.

7 Iraq

In the As Salam district of Tall 'Afar, a suicide bomber detonated a VBIED in a house being used by the military, killing four Iraqi soldiers and 13 civilians, wounding four soldiers and nine civilians, and damaging the targeted house and well as several civilian houses. No group claimed responsibility.

9 Iraq

In the Sha'ab District of northern Baghdad, assailants detonated an IED hidden inside a plastic bag in the Shiite Shalal market. A few minutes later, as civilians gathered at the scene, a roadside VBIED exploded, killing 13 civilians, wounding 46 others, and damaging several cars, shops, and market stalls. Although no group claimed responsibility, authorities suspect Sunni extremists of perpetrating this attack.

10 Iraq

In the Dora District of southern Baghdad, assailants detonated an IED placed underneath a car near a bakery, killing 11 civilians, wounding four others, and destroying the bakery. No group claimed responsibility.

10 Iraq

In various districts of Ba'qubah, Diyala, assailants, in separate attacks, fired upon and killed between eight and 12 civilians. No group claimed responsibility.

12 Iraq

In the Zayoona District of eastern Baghdad, assailants, arriving in police vehicles and some wearing police uniforms, stormed the offices of the Al-Sha'biyah television station, killing six employees, the station owner, two security guards, and two newscasters, while wounding two other employees, and causing unspecified damage to the station. No group claimed responsibility although Shiite militia members were suspected.

12 Iraq

In Ad Dulu'ya, Salah ad Din, assailants kidnapped 17 Shiite construction workers as they left work. On 13 October, near Ad Dulu'iyah, Salah ad Din, in an orchard, authorities found the bodies of the hostages bound and beheaded. No group claimed responsibility although it was widely believed Sunni extremists were responsible.

13 Iraq

Near Suwayrah, Wasit, assailants attacked a farm house, killing seven civilians and three children, all from the same family, and damaging their residence. No group claimed responsibility.

15 Iraq

Near As Suwayrah, assailants fired upon a residence, killing 10 civilians and damaging the home. No group claimed responsibility.

16 Iraq

Near the Al Fardous mosque in Hayy Ur District of northern Baghdad, a VBIED exploded in a popular market. Minutes later a suicide bomber detonated a VBIED near a Shiite funeral tent. Both incidents killed a total of 20 civilians, wounded between 17 and 27 others, and damaged the market and tent. No group claimed responsibility.

16 Iraq

In As Suwayrah, a VBIED exploded near the Al Rafedeen bank, killing 10 civilians, wounding 45 others, and damaging several shops and vehicles. No group claimed responsibility.

19 Iraq

In Al Khalis, Diyala, an IED exploded in a market, killing 17 civilians, wounding 34 others and several children, and damaging the market. No group claimed responsibility.

19 Iraq

In Mosul, a suicide bomber detonated the VBIED he was driving near the Abi-Tammam police station, killing 10 civilians and one police officer, wounding 17 civilians and eight police officers, and damaging the station and 42 civilian vehicles at a nearby gas station. Shortly after the suicide attack, assailants fired several mortar rounds at another police station, killing nine civilians. Islamic State in Iraq/Mujahidin Shura Council (DII/MSM) claimed responsibility.

19 Iraq

In Kirkuk, a suicide bomber detonated the VBIED he was driving outside a bank near soldiers waiting to pick up pay, killing four soldiers and eight civilians, wounding 70 other civilians, and damaging the bank, two military vehicles, and several shops nearby. No group claimed responsibility.

21 Iraq

In Mahmudiyah, Ninawa, assailants detonated five bicycle-borne IEDs in an outdoor market, then fired 12 mortar rounds at an unknown target, hitting a residential area and crowded outdoor market, killing 30 civilians and wounding between 50 and 70 others. Authorities found and defused a sixth bicycle bomb in a controlled explosion. No group claimed responsibility.

22 Iraq

In Ba'quba, Diyala, assailants detonated an IED near a convoy of buses carrying Shiite Muslim police recruits. The initial explosion caused light damage to one bus but no injuries. After detonating the IED, the assailants boarded the buses, killing 15 and wounding 24. Following the attack, the assailants placed one IED near each of the 15 dead recruits. United States military forces successfully defused all 15 IEDs. No group claimed responsibility for the attack.

26 Iraq

Near Ba'qubah, Diyala, assailants ambushed a group of Iraqi police officers, killing 28 officers and wounding 25 others. No group claimed responsibility.

27 Iraq

In Mosul, assailants attacked a police patrol, killing four police officers and eight civilians. No group claimed responsibility.

29 Iraq

In Al Basrah, assailants kidnapped 17 government employees and two government contractors who were on their way home from work. Their bodies were found the next day in Ash Shu`aybah. No group claimed responsibility.

29 Iraq

In Diyala, armed assailants fired upon and killed 25 police officers in an ambush. No group claimed responsibility.

30 Iraq

In Mudhafa Square on the perimeter of Sadr City, Baghdad, assailants detonated a roadside IED, killing 33 civilians, including several children, and wounding 65 others. The explosion tore through food stalls and kiosks, cutting down the victims who were gathered there looking for work. No group claimed responsibility, although it was widely believed that Sunni Islamic extremists were responsible.

31 Iraq

In the Shaab neighborhood, Hayy Ur District, of Baghdad, a suicide bomber detonated a VBIED at a Shiite wedding party, killing 19 children and four civilians, wounding 10 children and nine civilians, and damaging a small minibus parked nearby. No group claimed responsibility.

November

7 Iraq

In the predominantly Shiite Grai'at area of northern Baghdad, a suicide bomber detonated an IED inside a cafe, killing between 17 and 25 civilians, wounding 25 others, and damaging the cafe. No group claimed responsibility.

7 Iraq

In the predominantly Sunni Adhamiya District of northern Baghdad, assailants attacked the area with up to 12 mortar rounds, killing between seven and 12 civilians and wounding between 26 and 50 others. No group claimed responsibility.

10 Iraq

Near Al Yusufiyah, Babil, assailants wearing masks and using four cars attacked two houses, kidnapping 11 civilians and three children. Later the same day their bodies were found in a nearby field with multiple gunshot wounds. No group claimed responsibility.

11 Iraq

Near Al Latifiyah, Babil, assailants established a false checkpoint and stopped three minibuses carrying Shiite civilians traveling from Ad Diwaniyah. They then killed between 10 and 12 civilians and kidnapped between 13 and 68 others. No group claimed responsibility, although Sunni extremists are suspected of perpetrating this attack.

12 Iraq

In Nissur Square in western Baghdad, two suicide bombers wearing IEDs detonated the devices at a police commando recruitment center, killing 35 civilians, wounding 60 others, and damaging the police facility. The Islamic State of Iraq/Mujahidin Shura Council (DII/MSM) claimed responsibility.

13 Iraq

In the predominantly Shiite Sha'ab District of northern Baghdad, assailants detonated an IED left on board a minibus, killing between 10 and 19 civilian and one child, wounding 18 others civilians, and destroying the minibus. No group claimed responsibility.

14 Iraq

In the Sunni Shorja District of central Baghdad, assailants detonated a roadside VBIED near the Shorja market, killing 10 civilians, wounding 25 others, and damaging the market. No group claimed responsibility.

14 Iraq

In the Rusafa District of central Baghdad, assailants detonated a roadside VBIED targeting traffic between the city center and the Sadr City, killing 21 civilians, wounding 25 others, and damaging several cars. No group claimed responsibility.

15 Iraq

At the Al-Killani fuel station in central Baghdad, a VBIED exploded, killing 12 civilians, wounding 33 others, and damaging the station and six vehicles. No group claimed responsibility.

19 Iraq

In Al Hillah, Babil, a suicide bomber detonated his VBIED in a crowd of laborers after luring them to his van with promises of work, killing 22 civilians, wounding 49 others, and causing light damage to nearby shops. No group claimed responsibility.

19 Iraq

In the Mashtal District of eastern Baghdad, two VBIEDs and one IED exploded nearly simultaneously at a bus station, killing 11 civilians, wounding 51 others, and causing light damage to the station. No group claimed responsibility.

23 Iraq

In the Jamila vegetable market in Sadr City, Baghdad, assailants IEDs and five suicide VBIEDs. The assailants then launched mortars at the al Shahidein Square and Mudhaffer Square. The attacks were targeting stores selling religious CDs and electronics outlets. The coordinated attacks, which occurred within fifteen minutes of each other, killed 138 civilians, wounded 257 others, and caused unspecified damage. A sixth VBIED was found and defused before it could be detonated. No group claimed responsibility, although it was widely believed that Sunni Islamic extremists were responsible.

23 Iraq

In the predominantly Sunni Adhamiya District of Baghdad, assailants attacked residential areas, a market, and the shrine of the Sunni Imam Abu-Hanifah al-Nu'man with mortar rounds, killing 20 civilians, wounding five others, and causing unspecified damage. No group claimed responsibility.

24 Iraq

In Tall 'Afar, a suicide bomber detonated his explosives outside a car dealership and a VBIED exploded shortly thereafter, killing 22 people and wounding 26 others. The attack also damaged several vehicles. No group claimed responsibility.

24 Iraq

In Balad Ruz, Diyala, assailants kidnapped 22 farmers from two extended families. The armed assailants took the farmers to nearby fields and killed them. The next day, police found their bodies. No group claimed responsibility.

24 Iraq

In Al Basrah, assailants attacked a mosque with mortars, killing fifteen civilians and causing unspecified damage. No group claimed responsibility.

24 Iraq

In Al Qa'im, Al Anbar, assailants kidnapped 11 students who were on their way to Haditha. The students' bodies were found the following day. No group claimed responsibility.

25 Iraq

Near Ar Ramadi, assailants attacked members of the Abu Soda tribe with small arms and mortar fire, killing 15 tribal members, and burning several homes. No group claimed responsibility, although the Islamic State of Iraq/Mujahidin Shura Council was blamed for the attack.

26 Iraq

In the Sunni Adhamiya District of northern Baghdad, assailants attacked a residential neighborhood with at least six mortar rounds, killing 10 civilians, wounding 28 others, and causing unspecified damage. The mortar rounds were fired from Sadr City of eastern Baghdad, indicating the assailants were probably Shiite extremists.

December

2 Iraq

Near al-Wathba Square in central Baghdad, assailants detonated three VBIEDs nearly simultaneously at a popular food market, killing between 68 and 91 civilians, wounding up to 121 others and a businessman, and damaging the market, several shops, and at least 12 cars. No group claimed responsibility.

2 Iraq

North of Al Kut, Wasit, an assailant drove an empty fuel truck into a bus stop, killing between 18 and 20 civilians, wounding 15 others, and damaging the bus stop. No group claimed responsibility.

5 Iraq

In central Baghdad, assailants attacked a bus with machine guns and a hand grenade, killing 15 employees of the state-run Shiite Endowment Office (Waqf Office), wounding nine others, and damaging the bus. In the Adhamiya District of northern Baghdad, assailants detonated a VBIED against at least one vehicle transporting the dead and wounded, damaging the vehicle. No group claimed responsibility.

5 Iraq

In the Suleikh District of northern Baghdad, a suicide bomber detonated a VBIED in a crowd of 600 police cadets. Assailants then fired upon the group from nearby orchards, killing 11 cadets and wounding 12 others. No group claimed responsibility.

5 Iraq

In the Bayaa' District of southwestern Baghdad, assailants detonated a VBIED at the Wahed Huzairan gas station, killing 15 or 16 civilians, wounding between 25 and 30 others, and damaging the station. No group claimed responsibility.

6 Iraq

In the Maidan District of central Baghdad, assailants possibly attacked a market with several mortar rounds, killing between 10 and 15 civilians, wounding between 25 and 54 others, and damaging the market and several stores near a bus station. No group claimed responsibility.

8 Iraq

In southeast Baghdad, assailants attacked a predominantly Shiite residential neighborhood with 30 mortar rounds, killing between 20 and 22 civilians and several children, wounding up to 22 other civilians, and destroying seven houses. No group claimed responsibility.

12 Iraq

In Tayaran Square in central Baghdad, a suicide bomber using a minivan detonated a VBIED and a second VBIED exploded at a gathering area for Shiite day-laborers, killing 69 mostly Shiite civilians and seven police officers, wounding between 200 and 236 other civilians, and damaging two buildings, dozens of shops, and setting fire to 10 cars. Sunni extremists are suspected of perpetrating this attack.

13 Iraq

In the Shiite Kamaliya District of eastern Baghdad, assailants detonated a VBIED near a bus stop and across the street from the Shiite al-Rasoul Mosque, killing

11 Shiite civilians, wounding 27 others, and damaging the bus stop, several shops, and three cars. No group claimed responsibility.

13 Iraq

In the predominantly Shiite Jadida District of eastern Baghdad, assailants detonated two roadside VBIEDs near a gathering site for Shiite day laborers and the Sunni al-Samouri Mosque, killing nine Shiite civilians, two police officers, and one Christian civilian, wounding nine other Shiite civilians, three police officers, and one Christian civilian but causing no damage to the mosque. Ansar al-Sunnah claimed responsibility.

20 Iraq

In Jadriya District, Baghdad, a suicide bomber detonated a VBIED at a police checkpoint outside the gates of Baghdad University, killing between five and eight civilians and between three and six police officers and wounding between 21 and 23 civilians and between seven and nine police officers. The checkpoint and several nearby buildings were damaged in the attack. Islamic State of Iraq/Mujahidin Shura Council (DII/MSM) claimed responsibility.

21 Iraq

On Palestine Street in eastern Baghdad, a suicide bomber, standing in line with police recruits, detonated an IED, killing three police officers and 12 civilians, wounding 15 others, and causing light damage. Islamic State of Iraq/Mujahidin Shura Council (DII/MSM) claimed responsibility.

25 Iraq

In the predominantly Shiite New Baghdad District, at an open-air market, a VBIED detonated, killing ten civilians, wounding 15 others, and causing unspecified damage. No group claimed responsibility.

26 Iraq

In the Adhamiya District of Baghdad, a VBIED detonated, killing 20 civilians and wounding 35 others. The Islamic State of Iraq/Mujahidin Shura Council (DII/MSM) claimed responsibility.

26 Iraq

In the Bayaa' District, Baghdad, three VBIEDs detonated simultaneously, killing 16 civilians and wounding 70 others. No group claimed responsibility.

27 Iraq

On Palestine Street in northeastern Baghdad, assailants detonated a VBIED near an Iraqi Army checkpoint and the Nasaiyf Restaurant, killing 15 civilians, wounding 20 others, and damaging the checkpoint, four cars, the restaurant, and several shops. No group claimed responsibility.

28 Iraq

In the Zayyunah area of central Baghdad, assailants detonated a VBIED at a gas station near Shaab stadium where people were lined up to get kerosene, killing 10 civilians, wounding 25 others, and damaging the station. No group claimed responsibility.

28 Iraq

In central Baghdad, two roadside IEDs exploded at the Bab al-Sarji market, killing 11 civilians, wounding 43 others, and causing unspecified damage to the market. No group claimed responsibility.

30 Iraq

In Baghdad, assailants detonated at least two VBIEDs, killing 36 civilians and wounding 76 others. No group claimed responsibility.

30 Iraq

In Kufa, an Najaf, an assailant detonated a VBIED near a fish market, killing 27 Shia civilians and four children, wounding 58 civilians, and damaging the market. No group claimed responsibility.

South Asia

The 2006 overall tally of incidents and victims varied considerably across this region, as compared with that in 2005, with some countries showing notable changes. In this region, there were 3,654 incidents in 2006, fewer than the more than 4,000 in 2005; there were 19 percent more fatalities in 2006, rising to about 3,600 from roughly 3,000 in 2005; and the kidnapping victim total nose-dived, falling 63 percent, from nearly 33,500 in 2005 to 12,235 last year.

- With increased resistance against Afghan and coalition forces last year, incidents of terror rose in **Afghanistan** in 2006 by 50 percent, from nearly 500 in 2005 to approximately 750 last year. Three hundred of these incidents included police officials among the victims. Suicide attacks in 2006 climbed 370 percent to 80 from 17 the previous year, and the wounded rose 127 percent, reaching 2,025 in 2006 and compared with 890 in the 2005. Moreover, the number of reports including attacks on schools doubled in 2006 from 2005, to 61.
- Incidents in **Pakistan** fell nearly 20 percent in 2006, from 486 in 2005 to 390 but the count of dead and wounded increased—fatalities were up 14 percent from 338 to 387 in 2006, and the wounded up 80 percent, from 634 in 2005 to 1,140 in 2006. The perpetrators most often cited in open sources are the Balch tribal factions, the Balochistan Liberation Army (BLA), the Taliban, and al-Qa'ida.
- Incidents in **Bangladesh** were down 15 percent, falling to 86 from 102 in 2005 apparently because of the capture of Jamatul Mujahideen Bangladesh (JMB) leaders.
- Incidents in **India** were down 24 percent, dropping from 1,379 in 2005 to 1,045 last year. Despite the decline, 8 percent more noncombatants—1,256 individuals—were killed in 2006, injured victims were up, by 31 percent to 3,431, and kidnapping victim totals soared upward by 503 percent, from 282 to 1,701 last year. Incidents in *Jammu* and *Kashmir* dropped from 722 in 2005, to 621 in 2006, a 14 percent tumble. Fatalities in this area were down 33 percent, to 443 from 661, wounded victims decreased by about the same percentage, to just over 1,400, but kidnappings were up by 26 percent, rising from 60 to 76 last year. Grenade attacks in *Jammu* and *Kashmir*, mostly in urban areas, were up 89 percent to 161 attacks in 2006. The overall decline in incidents in this area may reflect an increase in local resistance toward subnational groups or constricted support for these groups by the Pakistani Inter-Services Intelligence Directorate (ISID).
- Both the number of incidents and victims fell across the board in **Nepal**, including a substantial falloff of 69 percent in kidnapping victims in 2006, from nearly 33,000 in 2005 to 10, 294 this past year. Incidents fell 14 percent from those in 2005, to 1,169 from 1,365, while fatalities dropped 46 percent, to 261 from 485, and the number wounded was lower by 21 percent, reaching 793 in 2006, as compared to more than

1,000 in 2005. The overall improvement is attributable to the political dialogue between the Maoists and government, which resulted in an April ceasefire and a November peace agreement.

- Incidents fell slightly, by 13 percent, in **Sri Lanka** in 2006 but ticked upward in the last half of the year after peace talks between LTTE and the government failed in April. Although there were fewer incidents, 235 in 2006, fatalities soared by 382 percent, from 130 to 627 last year. Wounded victims, 1,149 in 2006 as compared with 425 in 2005, increased by 170 percent.

Fifty-two Incidents of 10 or more Fatalities

Sixteen of these incidents occurred in India, and 15 incidents took place in Afghanistan. The largest and deadliest occurred on 11 July in Mumbai, India, where terrorists, widely believed to be members of Lashkar-e-Tayyiba (LT) terrorist group, simultaneously struck seven commuter trains, killing at least 203 and wounding nearly 900.

January

5 Afghanistan

In Tarin Kowt, Oruzgan Province, a suicide bomber detonated an explosive device in a market near the provincial headquarters, killing one police officer and 10 civilians, wounding one police officer and 49 civilians, and causing unspecified damage to the market. The Taliban claimed responsibility.

14 Nepal

In Thankot, Kathmandu District, assailants attacked the Area Police Office, killing at least 11 security personnel and wounding several others. No group claimed responsibility, although it was widely believed the Communist Party of Nepal (Maoist)/United People's Front was responsible.

16 Afghanistan

In Spin Buldak, Kandahar Province, a suicide bomber on a motorcycle detonated a VBIED in a crowd of people leaving a wrestling match, killing 22 civilians, wounding 27 others, and causing unspecified damage. No group claimed responsibility.

31 Nepal

In Tansen, Palpa District, assailants used bombs and guns to attack several government and military facilities in the district headquarters, killing 17 police officers and seven Royal Nepalese Army (RNA) soldiers, wounding 10 police officers and seven soldiers, and abducting at least 20 police officers, six RNA soldiers, two government officials, and one government employee. The attack also damaged the District Jail, one RNA barracks, the District Administration Office, and several other government buildings. By 7 February 2006, the assailants had released all of the abductees. The Communist Party of Nepal (Maoist)/United People's Front claimed responsibility.

February

5 Pakistan

In Kolpur, Balochistan Province, assailants detonated explosive devices on a bus, killing 13 civilians, wounding 20 others, and damaging the bus. No group claimed responsibility.

6 India

In the Kottacheur area, Dantewada, assailants detonated a landmine under a Nagaland Armed Police (NAP) vehicle traveling through a forest, killing 10 police officers, wounding 8 others, and damaging their vehicle. No group claimed responsibility, but it was widely believed the Communist Party of India-Maoist (CPI-Maoist) was responsible.

7 Afghanistan

In Kandahar, a suicide bomber on a motorcycle detonated an IED outside a police station, killing seven police officers and six civilians, wounding five police officers and eight civilians, and damaging the police station and several nearby vehicles. The Taliban claimed responsibility.

9 Pakistan

In Hangu, North-West Frontier Province, a suicide bomber walked into a procession of Shiite Muslims celebrating the Ashura holy day and detonated an IED strapped to his body, killing approximately 32 civilians. This incident sparked retaliatory violence that escalated into a two-day battle between rival Muslim sects and included the shooting deaths of four civilians on a bus and four civilian truck drivers. The fighting left approximately 91 civilians from both sides wounded. Several businesses in the local bazaar were destroyed in the violence. No group claimed responsibility but the initial assailant was widely believed to be a Sunni Islamic extremist.

28 India

Near Eklagoda village, in the Darmagura area, Dantewada, assailants ambushed five trucks carrying anti-Maoist campaigners returning from a 'Salwa Judum,' or peace movement, killing 55 civilians, injuring at least 40 others, and kidnapping approximately 125 others. The assailants detonated a landmine under one of the trucks and set fire to the remaining four, destroying all five trucks. No group claimed responsibility, although it was widely believed the Communist Party of India-Maoist (CPI-Maoist) was responsible.

28 Nepal

On the border of Arghakhanchi and Palpa Districts, assailants fired upon a security patrol, killing nine Royal Nepalese Army soldiers and one police officer and wounding two civilians. No group claimed responsibility, although it was widely believed the Communist Party of Nepal (Maoist)/United People's Front was responsible.

March

7 India

In Varanasi, assailants detonated three bombs in a coordinated attack, killing at least 15 civilians, injuring at least 101 civilians, and damaging a Hindu temple and a railway station. The first explosion occurred near Benaras Hindu University at the Sankat Mochan temple, which at the time was occupied by hundreds of Hindu worshipers. The two explosions that followed occurred at the Varanasi Cantonment Railway Station. One bomb exploded inside the Shivganga Express train, which was scheduled to leave for Delhi, while the other exploded in a waiting hall. Authorities defused an additional six bombs found throughout the city, including one at a restaurant frequented by foreigners. Lashkar-e-Kahar claimed responsibility, although authorities believed Lashkar-e-Tayyiba (LT) was responsible.

10 Pakistan

In Dera Bugti, Balochistan, a vehicle carrying a large wedding party struck a landmine, killing 28 civilians, including an undisclosed number of children, wounding seven others, and damaging the vehicle. No group claimed responsibility.

20 Nepal

In Bhakundebesi Chhatrebas, Kabhre Palanchok District, assailants and security forces engaged in a gun fight when security personnel arrived in the area to restore the drinking water supply that the assailants had cut off, killing as many as 13 security personnel and injuring three others and one civilian. No group claimed responsibility, although it was widely believed the Communist Party of Nepal (Maoist)/United People's Front was responsible.

21 Nepal

In Birtamod, Jhapa District, assailants simultaneously attacked the Area Police Office (APO) and the Traffic Police Office, killing nine police officers and one civilian, wounding 21 police officers and two prisoners in custody at the (APO), and damaging both facilities. Prior to launching their attack, the assailants obstructed nearby roads by setting fire to two trucks at Harchana Bridge and Deunia Bridge. No group claimed responsibility, although it was widely believed the Communist Party of Nepal (Maoist)/United People's Front was responsible.

25 India

In Ghodagaon village, Kanker, Chhattisgarh, a landmine exploded, killing 13 businesspeople, injuring four others, and damaging three vehicles in their convoy. The Communist Party of India-Maoist (CPI-Maoist) claimed responsibility.

April

5 Nepal

Between 5 April 2006 and 6 April 2006, from 9:00 PM to 3:00 AM, in Malangawa N.P. and Nawalpur, Sarlahi District, assailants launched simultaneous attacks using sophisticated weapons and explosives on security installations, government offices, and the Arjun Band barracks of the Royal Nepalese Army, killing 10 security personnel, 6 police officers, and two civilians; wounding 27 other security personnel and 6 civilians; and causing five district government offices and one district police office to catch fire. Following the attacks, the assailants kidnapped 11 police officers and 14 government officials. On 20 April 2006, in an unknown area in Sindhuli District, Nepal, the assailants released 19 of the hostages, not including the Chief District Officer. On 11 May 2006, in Kehani, Udayapur District, Nepal, assailants released the Chief District Officer. No group claimed responsibility, although authorities believed the Communist Party of Nepal (Maoist)/United People's Front was responsible.

11 Pakistan

In Karachi, one or two suicide bombers detonated an undetermined number of IEDs during a sunset celebration of the birth of the prophet Mohammad, killing three Sunni clerics and 55 Sunni civilians and wounding 100 other civilians. No group claimed responsibility.

11 Sri Lanka

In Thambalagamuva, Eastern Province, assailants detonated a claymore mine as a bus carrying Sri Lankan Navy sailors drove by, killing 11 sailors and the civilian bus driver, wounding nine sailors, and damaging the bus. Three British civilians were wounded when their vehicle was hit by the bus and damaged during the attack. No group claimed responsibility, although it was widely believed the Liberation Tigers of Tamil Eelam (LTTE) was responsible.

12   Sri Lanka

In Trincomalee, Eastern Province, assailants detonated an IED in a market, killing 15 civilians and one soldier and wounding 50 civilians. The IED was affixed to a bicycle. Rioting erupted after the incident, resulting in an indefinite number of civilian wounded. No group claimed responsibility, although it was widely believed the Liberation Tigers of Tamil Eelam (LTTE) was responsible.

16   India   - 4/16/2006

In Dantewada, Chhattisgarh, assailants hijacked a passenger bus. They then drove to and fired upon a police post, killing at least 10 police officers, wounding four others, and causing light damage to the police post. The assailants also infiltrated the post and stole a large number of firearms and blocked the highway to prevent police reinforcements. No group claimed responsibility, although it is widely believed that the Communist Party of India-Maoist (CPI-M) was responsible.

25   India

In Manikonta village, Dantewada, assailants killed 15 civilians and kidnapped 52 others. The attackers then placed at least one improvised explosive device (IED) in the pile of dead victims. They detonated the IED when police arrived, causing no injuries or damage. No group claimed responsibility, although it is widely believed that the Communist Party of India-Maoist was responsible.

25   Sri Lanka

In Colombo, a suicide bomber detonated a body-worn explosive, killing three civilians and eight soldiers and wounding 26 other civilians and soldiers. The principal target was the commander of the Sri Lankan Army (SLA), who was wounded in the attack. No group claimed responsibility, although it was widely believed the Liberation Tigers of Tamil Eelam (LTTE) was responsible.

30   India

In Udhampur, Jammu and Kashmir, assailants kidnapped 15 Hindu civilians, killing 13 of the victims and releasing two. No group claimed responsibility, although authorities believed Hizbul-Mujahedin (HM) was responsible.

May

1   India

In Doda, Jammu and Kashmir, armed assailants kidnapped and fired upon a group of Hindu civilians, killing 22 civilians and wounding six others. Lashkar-e-Tayyiba (LT) claimed responsibility.

16 India

In Gadchiroli, Maharashtra, a landmine exploded under a van transporting people from a wedding, killing 12 civilians and destroying the van. No group claimed responsibility, although it is widely believed that the Communist Party of India-Maoist (CPI-Maoist) was responsible.

17 Afghanistan

In Musa Qal'eh, Helmand Province, assailants opened fire on the police and government headquarters building, starting a firefight that killed twelve police officers, wounded five others, and damaged the building. The Taliban claimed responsibility.

28 Sri Lanka

At night, in Welikanda, North Central Province, assailants fired upon a group of workers at an irrigation construction site, killing 12 men and wounding two others. The victims were tied together before being killed execution-style. No group claimed responsibility, although it was widely believed the Liberation Tigers of Tamil Eelam (LTTE) was responsible.

June

1 India

In Singhbhum, police officers and members of the Central Reserve Police Force (CRPF) located and safely defused an IED placed in a school. As the security forces were leaving the scene, a landmine exploded under their vehicle, killing six police officers and six members of the CPRF while destroying the vehicle. No group claimed responsibility, although it is widely believed that the Communist Party of India - Maoist (CPI-Maoist) was responsible.

12 India

In Kulgam, Anantnag, Jammu and Kashmir, assailants dressed as members of the Indian military and riding in military vehicles kidnapped one soldier, one Indian civilian, and 11 Nepalese civilians and at least one child. After torturing the hostages, including cutting off the soldier's hand, the soldier was beheaded while the civilians were fired upon, killing seven Nepalese civilians, one Indian civilian and one Nepalese child, and wounding four other Nepalese civilians. The Hizbul-Mujahedin (HM) and Lashkar-e-Tayyiba (LT) claimed joint responsibility for the attack.

15 Sri Lanka

In Anuradhapura, North Central Province, assailants detonated two claymore mines targeting a civilian passenger bus, killing 15 children and 49 civilians, wounding 87 civilians, and damaging the bus. No group claimed responsibility, although it was widely believed the Liberation Tigers of Tamil Eelam (LTTE) was responsible.

July

11 India

On 11 July 2006, between 6:24 PM and 6:35 PM, in Mumbai, assailants detonated seven of eight improvised explosive devices (IEDs) planted in the overhead storage areas in the first class compartments of seven commuter trains, killing 203 civilians and at least six children, wounding 863 civilians and at least 27 children, and causing damage to seven trains. Authorities located and safely defused the eighth IED, causing no additional injuries or damage. Although an offshoot of the Students Islamic Movement of India (SIMI) calling itself Gujarat Revenge claimed responsibility, it was widely believed Lashkar-e-Tayyiba (LT) was responsible.

17 India

In Dantewada, assailants fired upon two police stations to draw away security forces from the Errabore Relief Camp. Soon after the police left, the assailants attacked the camp, firing upon civilians, assaulting them with bladed weapons, setting them on fire, detonating explosives, and setting homes on fire, killing 26 civilians and three children, wounding at least 80 civilians, kidnapping at least 23 others, and destroying at least 20 homes and damaging two police stations. The Communist Party of India-Maoist (CPI-Maoist) claimed responsibility.

22 Afghanistan

In Kandahar, a suicide bomber drove his car into a Canadian military patrol vehicle and detonated a VBIED, killing two Canadian soldiers and wounding 10 Afghan civilians and eight soldiers. Approximately thirty minutes later, after a crowd had gathered on the site, a suicide bomber in the crowd detonated explosives he had attached to himself, killing 10 civilians and wounding 25 others. The Taliban claimed responsibility.

August

3 Afghanistan -

In Panjva'i, Kandahar Province, an assailant detonated a VBIED in a crowded marketplace, killing 21 civilians, including an unspecified number of children, wounding 13 civilians, most of them children, and causing unspecified damage to the marketplace. The target of the assailant was a convoy of International Security Assistance Force vehicles, which suffered no damage or casualties. No group claimed responsibility, although it was widely believed the Taliban was responsible.

3 Sri Lanka

In Muttur, North Eastern Province, assailants fired mortar rounds, which hit an Arabic school, killing 10 civilians, wounding approximately 20 others, and causing unspecified damage. No group claimed responsibility, but it was widely believed that the Liberation Tigers of Tamil Eelam (LTTE) was responsible.

4 Sri Lanka

In Muttur, North Eastern Province, assailants fired upon and killed 17 Sri Lankan aid workers who were employees of the French humanitarian group Action Against Hunger. Most of the victims were killed execution-style. No group claimed responsibility.

28 Afghanistan

In Lashkar Gah, Helmand Province, a suicide bomber targeting the former Helmand police chief entered a crowded marketplace and detonated an IED attached to himself, killing 16 children, the former police chief, the former chief's bodyguard, and four civilians, wounding 43 other civilians, and damaging the marketplace. The Taliban claimed responsibility.

28 Sri Lanka

Near Sampur, Trincomalee, North Eastern Province, assailants fired artillery shells and mortar rounds, killing 23 civilians and 12 soldiers and injuring 106 civilians. No group claimed responsibility, but it was widely believed the Liberation Tigers of Tamil Eelam (LTTE) was responsible.

September

8 Afghanistan

In Kabul, a suicide bomber detonated a VBIED against a US military Humvee roughly 100 yards from the US Embassy. The explosion killed two US soldiers and 16 Afghan civilians, wounded two other US soldiers and 29 Afghan civilians, destroyed one US Humvee, and blew out the windows of many nearby houses and buildings. The Taliban claimed responsibility.

8 India

In Malegaon, Nasik, Maharashtra, assailants detonated at least two IEDs hidden in bicycles in a Muslim cemetery and mosque, killing at least 31 civilians and wounding at least 125 more. The victims were celebrating the Muslim holy day of Shab-e-Bara'at. No group claimed responsibility, although police suspected Lashkar-e-Tayyiba (LT) was responsible and arrested members of the Students Islamic Movement of India.

17 Afghanistan

In Heart, a suicide bomber detonated a VBIED as Herat's deputy police chief was standing outside a mosque. The explosion killed six civilians, four police officers, and one child, wounded 13 civilians, four police officers, and one child, and damaged the mosque. The deputy police chief was among the wounded. No group claimed responsibility.

18 Sri Lanka

In Pottuvil, Ampara District, North Eastern Province, assailants with primitive weapons killed 10 Muslim civilians and wounded one other. No group claimed responsibility, but it was widely believed that the Liberation Tigers of Tamil Eelam (LTTE) was responsible.

22 Afghanistan

In Kandahar, a bomb planted on the side of a road exploded as a bus full of Afghan construction workers passed, killing 19, wounding three others, and destroying the bus. After the explosion, assailants fired upon the burning bus. No group claimed responsibility, although it was widely believed the Taliban was responsible.

26 Afghanistan

In Lashkar Gah, Helmand, a suicide bomber wearing an IED attacked a security post near a crowded mosque and the provincial governor's house. The explosion killed 12 civilians, three police officers, and three Afghan soldiers and wounded 12 civilians, three police officers, and three soldiers. When the explosion occurred, hundreds of Afghans were gathered to seek permission for pilgrimages to Mecca, Saudi Arabia. The Taliban claimed responsibility.

30 Afghanistan

In Kabul, as Ministry of Interior employees and civilians were gathered around the main gate to enter the compound, a suicide bomber detonated an IED that killed one child, seven civilians, and four police officers and wounded at least 42 other people, including unspecified numbers of government employees, civilians, and police officers. Damage was reported to the Ministry of Interior building and several local businesses. The Taliban claimed responsibility.

October

6 India

In North Cachar Hills, Assam, assailants fired upon four vehicles used by the Railroad Special Protection Force (RSPF) and other railroad employees, killing seven RSPF officers and five civilians, wounding three other civilians, damaging the four vehicles, and stealing the RSPF firearms. No group claimed responsibility.

16 Sri Lanka

In Digampathaha, Habarane, North Central Province, at a transit point for security personnel, suicide bombers detonated a VBIED, killing 120 unarmed sailors and wounding 150 others. Of the 24 buses in the area, between 12 and 15 buses sustained damage. Some of the sailors were returning home for vacation and others were returning for duty. No group claimed responsibility, although it was widely believed the Liberation Tigers of Tamil Eelam (LTTE) was responsible.

27 Afghanistan

In Tarin Kowt, Oruzgan Province, a landmine exploded when it was run over by a passenger bus, killing 14 civilians, including several children, wounding three others, and damaging the bus. No group claimed responsibility, although it was widely believed the Taliban was responsible.

November

8 Sri Lanka

In Vakarai, North Eastern Province, assailants fired upon military forces from civilian areas, inciting retaliatory artillery fire from the military that killed 6 infants and 39 civilians, wounded 200 others, and damaged a school that was being used as a refugee shelter. No group claimed responsibility, although it was widely believed the Liberation Tigers of Tamil Eelam (LTTE) was responsible.

26 Afghanistan

In Orgun-e Kalan, Paktika Province, a suicide bomber entered a restaurant frequented by a local police chief and militia chief and detonated an IED as the pair ate together. The explosion killed 15 civilians and wounded the police chief, the militia chief, three of their bodyguards, and 20 civilians. The restaurant and several other shops in the bazaar were damaged. The Taliban claimed responsibility.

December

2 India

In Palamau, Jharkhand, a landmine exploded, killing 16 police officers and destroying their vehicle. The Communist Party of India-Maoist (CPI-Maoist) claimed responsibility.

18 Afghanistan

In Panjva'i, Kandahar Province, assailants killed 26 civilians suspected of collaborating with the North American Treaty Organization (NATO) forces. The Taliban claimed responsibility.

Western Hemisphere

The number of incidents occurring remained steady—the tally of 826 in 2006 was just below the 868 incidents recorded for 2005. Ninety percent of the incidents—nearly 800 of them—were conducted in **Colombia** by terrorist organizations and paramilitary groups. The Revolutionary Armed Forces of Colombia (FARC), the largest terrorist and insurgent group in **Colombia**, was most often reported as the assailants in these attacks.

- Across the hemisphere, there was a decrease in fatalities, kidnappings, and wounded, a 25 to 30 percent range of decline in each victim category. In 2006, according to open-sources, 556 individuals were killed, another 688 wounded, and 353 kidnapped.

Three Incidents of 10 or More Fatalities

All three incidents were in Colombia.

- On 27 February, in Rivera, Huila, armed assailants attacked a group of government officials at a lunchtime meeting in the Los Gabrieles club, killing nine council members, two police officers, and one guard, wounding two council members and one police officer, and probably damaging the restaurant. No group claimed responsibility, although it was widely believed that the FARC was responsible.

- On or about 17 June 2006, in Balboa, Cauca assailants killed two children and nine civilians. No group claimed responsibility.

- On 12 June at about 5:00 PM, in Rio Sucio, Choco, assailants entered a camp and kidnapped at least 35 woodcutters. Four or five were able to escape immediately, and the Colombian military found 13 bodies believed to have been among the 35 kidnapped. On or about 17 June 2006, other victims were released. No group claimed responsibility, although it is widely believed that the FARC was responsible.